THE GREATEST FOOTBALLER YOU NEVER SAW

Paul McGuigan (or Guigsy as he is known worldwide) is the bass player of Oasis. Since childhood he has been a fervent Manchester City supporter, and through his support has learned much about life in general. A promising player himself, he had trials with Oldham and Stockport among others before a knee injury cut short his football aspirations. While on tour with the band in America, Guigsy came across a magazine article about Robin Friday and was inspired to find out more about the genius maverick player. This book is the result of his investigations.

Paolo Hewitt began writing for *Melody Maker* at the tender age of 19, moving on to the *NME* two years later. A highly respected music writer, he is the author of four books. One, *Heaven's Promise*, was the first novel to document the acid house scene in Britain. The others, *The Jam: A Beat Concerto*, *Small Faces: The Young Mod's Forgotten Story* and *Getting High: The Adventures of Oasis*, are all best-selling music biographies. He lives in north London and supports Spurs, Woking and Napoli. He has no idea what he would do if any of them were to meet in a major game.

the greatest footballer you never saw

THE ROBIN FRIDAY STORY

Paul McGuigan
and Paolo Hewitt

MAINSTREAM
PUBLISHING
EDINBURGH AND LONDON

Reprinted, 2007

First published in Great Britain in 1997 by
MAINSTREAM PUBLISHING COMPANY (EDINBURGH) LTD
7 Albany Street
Edinburgh EH1 3UG

ISBN 9781840181081

Reprinted 1997 (twice), 1998, 2004, 2005, 2006

A catalogue record for this book
is available from the British Library

Printed and bound in Great Britain by
Cox & Wyman Ltd

For all of Robin's family

Contents

Sometimes you'd think that he wasn't interested in football, but he was. It was just his way. He could be very laid-back. Often you'd read in the papers that there was a change when he got on the pitch. I'm not saying he was laid-back all the time, because he was a nutcase anyway. He was always rowing, always getting into rucks, even off the pitch. If he was in the pub and it went off, he would be there. He was a handful but he wasn't a liberty-taker is what I'm trying to say.

Tony Friday, 1997

Foreword

First, a winning title from Guigsy and Paolo; it says it all. Not a lot of people did get the opportunity to see Robin Friday play. He had a few seasons at Reading in the old Fourth Division and one at Cardiff in the old Second, retiring from the game when he was, by today's standards, not that far past the 'promising youngster' category.

He wasn't a player who seared into my consciousness as a football crazy kid, but I do remember the name. I grew up scanning team lists in *Goal, Shoot* and the Sunday papers like I scanned the pop charts, displaying that near autistic obsessiveness that characterises many young and not-so-young boys from these islands. It was a name which struck out for its appealing associations, like Derek Posse of Millwall a few years earlier. Maybe your childhood and adolescent subconscious leanings towards certain names, such as 'Friday' and 'Posse', shape your future behaviour and attitudes.

But I knew nothing of Robin Friday until Paolo, with his customary infectious enthusiasm, started telling me about this guy who played for Reading and was brilliant and didn't give a fuck. While I was ignorant of the player and the person, I instantly recognised the archetype: the monstrously gifted talent with a cavalier spirit and a hedonistic urge to live life to the full. In other words, someone gloriously unsuited to the discipline of professional sport. George Best, shadowed as a reference point in this book, was perhaps the patron saint of the breed, but he was just so shockingly brilliant that it was impossible for him not to rule the world. Best would go on to fulfil his potential, gracing the green of Hibernian Football Club, after a promising career with various provincial outfits in the English Leagues.

In Scotland, we've produced many such wayward talents. At the first Hibs–Hearts game I ever attended, the mighty Greens were firm favourites to win. They lost 3–1. The reason was this decrepit-looking guy in the middle of the park whom nobody could get the ball from. I remember booing this geriatric Jambo bastard and subsequently getting into a row from my dad, who told me that the guy was Willie Hamilton, and that he was The Man. Hamilton had been a Hibs hero of the past and had returned to Edinburgh after a spell in the south. He was described by none other than the late, great Jock Stein as the best player he had ever seen. It was Stein, in his brief period as Hibs manager a few years earlier, who managed to get the best out of Willie.

Like many such personalities, Hamilton thrived on the big occasion. Back in '67 he gave Ferenc Puskas a footballing lesson as Hibs beat Real Madrid 2–0 at The Stadium. It was the first game overseas the European Champions had lost for ages and their first ever defeat on British soil. A few days later Hamilton went to Ibrox to do the same to his great kindred spirit, Jim Baxter, as the Greens came out 4–2 winners over Rangers. Hamilton, though, won only one Scotland cap, against Finland in 1965. Like Robin Friday, he worked in the building trade (Willie was a brickie, Robin an asphalter). A sadder similarity was that both men were to have short lives, Hamilton's death in Canada occurring only ten years after his sole representative honour.

Rather than indulge in bullshit pseudo-psychological speculation about Robin Friday's motivations, or ghoulishly chart his decline, the authors give Robin's tale the dignity his skills and spirit deserve. They choose to let the people close to the man tell his story in their own words. My favourite passage comes from former Reading coach Maurice Evans who took Friday aside and told him: 'Robin, if you would just settle down for three or four years you could play for England.' The player replied: 'Yeah, but I've had a far better time than you've ever had in your life.' (This was an echo of the now-famous George Best incident, when a waiter interviewed him in a hotel room where the bed was decorated by Miss World, bottles of champagne and piles of money. The waiter was there to find out where it had all gone wrong for George.) To his great credit and honesty, Maurice Evans was big enough to consider Friday's retort and admit, 'That may be right'.

Things have changed since Robin Friday graced Reading in the 1970s. In today's game cash is now the undisputed king. The media focus is almost exclusively on the richer clubs. The pressure on fans, especially younger ones, is to become glory hunters: mercenaries following the highest-paid and most celebrated clubs. This means that the fans become celebrators of a club's achievements rather than supporters of the club of their community. There is an important difference. The celebrator will 'follow' the club, buy the merchandise, and, of course, read the obligatory bland star biography, ghost-written by some local or national newsman where every player is made to sound like Oscar Wilde on valium.

That's why Paolo and Guigsy's book is so timely. It's more than the best English football biography I've read, because it gives you a real flavour of the player, the rich and complex person that he was, the game itself, and the times. It's worth a million of the Gary Lineker-style biogs in print because it is a *real* football biography, rather than a mundane stocking-filler that publishers generally flog to sheep about the mercenaries who've already been fleecing them for a couple of seasons. It's more than that. It deserves to be widely read because it challenges us to reaffirm what the true essence of the beautiful game is – and what it isn't: greedy players, egotistical corporate chairmen and yuppie, glory-hunting-by-proxy supporters.

Yeah, perhaps not a lot of us did get the chance to see Robin Friday play, but those who did are just that wee bit more enriched as a result. And that's what it's all about.

Irvine Welsh
August 1997

Introduction

Yesterday, in the Ruislip Crematorium where Robin Friday is commemorated, the weather was hot, the aptly named Peace Gardens, where a rose bush now marks his name, silent. Few people passed by and those that did were too lost in their own memories to shatter the vast calm.

I have to say I found this tranquillity incongruous. If we had discovered one thing on our journey into the life and character of Robin Friday, it was that noise followed him everywhere. It erupted from the delirious crowds saluting another of his wonder goals. It surrounded him in the pubs and clubs he frequented on a regular basis. And it followed him home where the records he adored were always cranked up to full volume. Noise, noise, noise. Now there is just silence.

At such times – when visiting the dead – it is nearly impossible for the phrase 'I truly hope he/she is looking down on me', not to enter the mind. But this is a cliché that should be avoided as skilfully as Robin evaded the unruly lunges of defenders determined to damage him.

The thought I found inescapable after a year of studying the man was the almost surreal nature of my first contact with the name Robin Friday. This took place in a country that Robin never visited, originated from a writer whose work to date I was unfamiliar with and was shown to me by the bass player of the most successful group in the world. I speak of America, Graham Wray and Paul McGuigan.

It happened in March 1996 when I found myself reporting for

Select magazine on Oasis in America. Paul, or Guigsy as he is better known, placed in front of me an issue of *Goal* magazine and said, 'Read this article.'

I did. Four times. The story that Graham Wray had written told of an almost mythical player whose skills alone would have been enough to prompt the most serious of enquiries. The fact that Robin also led a pop star lifestyle within a magical world of girls, adoration and stimulants, beggared belief.

As we were soon to discover, Robin Friday was one of the most skilful players ever to have originated from this country. And it is not only the authors who firmly believe in this statement.

To attribute a player with such an accolade means that he has to possess one key element to align with his talent; that element is vision. Robin possessed it in abundance. Many of the people we spoke to talked about him having 'eyes in the back of his head'. Robin was always 'three or four steps ahead of the others'. It was the other side of his life, the carousing, the refusal of sobriety that seemed to mitigate against real recognition of his vast achievements.

Robin Friday was a natural goalscorer but his play was not constrained by the selfishness that is vital to a striker's temperament. He found nearly as much happiness in making goals for others simply because he was a warrior who would do anything to win.

That he was often victorious has everything to do with his phenomenal ball control ('Forget Shearer,' says one interviewee), dribbling skills and a shooting power aligned to devastating and instinctive accuracy. He was as responsible as one individual can be within a team unit for Reading's promotion to the then Third Division in 1976. Naturally, the Reading crowd adored him. Not only for his skills, not only for his devil-may-care nature but for his absolute refusal to bow down to anyone. On and off the pitch, Robin went his own way, gleefully sticking two fingers up to the world. He was, as that Super Furry Animals single stated, the man who didn't give a fuck. He was also in love with life, embracing it totally and fully.

Hugely talented, naturally skilful, that attitude translated itself onto the pitch where Robin was irresistible. He kissed policemen, kissed defenders at corners, grabbed people's testicles (the late Bobby Moore was but one player to have experienced The Hand of Robin), argued with referees and, at Cardiff, flicked V signs at goalkeepers. He made it possible for the Reading faithful to watch top-flight skills in a Fourth Division ground by doing things with the ball that no Reading player, past or present, has been able to match. And he did so with a cheerful smile and a buoyant nature that meant no demand from the crowd was too big for him.

Robin would spend hours signing autographs or scrounging match tickets for others. It was the people, his own kind, that he placed first, the people that he would come running to for true recognition of his skills and the people he preferred to hang out with. That many of them were scallywags meant little to Robin. Far better their company than that of the directors and the majority of his team-mates. Robin was a people's footballer because he never ever, as his brother points out, took liberties, and that spirit was relayed to them. Plus he played the game as most of us believe it should be played. With flair, élan, style and true beauty.

Yet, strangely, for a man of his immense talents, Robin Friday was a tough, hard-working player. When he took to the pitch he did so with a passion for winning so immense that it easily sustained his huge appetite for attack and defence play.

Nor did he shirk the physical side of the game. At a time when players such as Ron 'Chopper' Harris or Norman 'Bite Yer Legs' Hunter were being nationally celebrated for their 'ability' to scythe down opponents, Robin stood his ground. And he did so without any protection. Five minutes into every game his socks would be rolled down and his huge legs exposed as defenders hurtled into him, their studs scraping down his shins, their boots hammering into his bones. He simply shrugged them off. Or, if they got really insulting, decked them when no one was looking.

The following week as his Reading manager Charlie Hurley anxiously examined his wounds, Robin would look up and say, 'Fuck 'em, boss, I'm playing.' And boy did he play.

There was scarcely a match report that Guigsy and I scoured from the *Reading Evening Post* (116 games, 53 goals) that did not mention his name. It was usually in conjunction with a piece of outlandish skill or detailed yet another heated moment between Robin and the ref or Robin and his opponents.

In the case of the former, Robin regularly saw his name enter the referee's small black book. In the case of the latter Robin used everything at his disposal to unnerve the opposition.

Why then does Robin Friday remain an unknown? How could such a talent not play top-flight football? Why was he denied the England shirt that everyone thinks he had the right to pull on?

There is one obvious reason for his obscure status. Football in the '70s was not subject to today's media frenzy. Back in Robin's days as a pro (1973–76) football was still, in Alan Hudson's memorable phrase, the working-man's ballet. It was the working class that had to endure substandard conditions, crap food, hooliganism. Directors' boxes? All seated stadiums? Unthinkable.

In the '70s you were lucky to see highlights from five matches televised over a weekend. The papers only reported on First Division players. Had Robin been born in 1972 the media would have elevated him to such a position that the national pastime today would concern itself with the relative skills of Gazza and Robin.

That is one reason for his current lowly status. Another is that Robin Friday played life as he did football. As a free spirit. He could not distinguish between the two.

Blessed with awesome stamina, he ran riot outside football. He danced naked in clubs, naked in pubs. He openly smoked spliff and dropped pills. He caroused until late at night and would then return to his flat and crank his beloved music up until dawn. Girls flocked to him and he couldn't resist. Men rushed to buy him drinks and he could not resist.

Robin Friday did not have the willpower or the inclination to say no. He loved the crack, loved leading a pop star's life where everything you want suddenly becomes available. He was as flamboyant in front of the faithful at Elm Park as he was for the clientele of the Boar's Head, a pub, incidentally, he was banned from ten times.

Scouts find out about such things. All those First Division managers who sat in admiration of him at Reading's Elm Park ground backed off from his reputation.

There was only one manager who was able to be the Ferguson to his Cantona, the Venables to his Gazza. And that was Reading's manager, Charlie Hurley. He protected Robin as best he could but even he was taken to the limit, forced to let him go.

There is a theory that the horrendous accident that Robin suffered whilst working on a building site – he was impaled on a spike – formed the basis for these wild urges. There may be some truth in that. But it is not the only truth.

Robin was brought up in a close-knit working-class family who gave him and his twin brother Tony a love so absolute that a great confidence was instilled in the pair of them. The Friday brothers were never afraid to go their own way.

So it was that Robin, his fierce individualism coursing through his veins, always stood out from the crowd. He was the first to wear hippy clothing round his way. He was the first to get out of the estate. The first white man many could think of to marry a Caribbean girl called Maxine at 16 years of age and then have a daughter, Nicola, with her. This at a time when Enoch Powell, not to mention most of the Acton estate Robin lived in, wanted non-white citizens sent 'home'.

Like every artist, Robin was different. Like every strong individual who holds out for what they believe to be right, there is always a price to pay. I think it hurt Robin badly that people viewed him as a lout. A talented player, for sure, but a lout none the less. No one really credited him with any intelligence. He was too bawdy, too crude, never spoke proper Queen's English.

It was that kind of prejudice, so prevalent in this country, that got to him. Robin's fierce sense of fair play dictated that the way you look or speak should never obscure your achievements. But that's precisely what happened to him.

After moving to Cardiff and getting off to a great start, it soon became apparent that it was not just the opposition who were out to contain him but referees as well. For Robin, a scrupulously honest man in work and play, that was dishonesty at its worst. Football, sport indeed, should be the great equaliser of class and race. Once it is tilted away from absolute fairness then a player like Robin stands no chance. He quickly becomes disillusioned.

And I think that was one of the main reasons – along with isolation from his family – as to why he gave up on football.

Of course his problems were further exacerbated by his desire to obliterate them through stimulants rather than face up to them. He would rather get out of his mind than examine it, and his body started giving out warning signals.

His stay at Cardiff (25 games, 7 goals) was not particularly happy. Yet even in this brief period he still made a huge impact. I know this because in 1996, in a Cardiff bar at three in the morning, there were some lads starting to get a little bit feisty with myself and Guigsy. Just as things were starting to turn a ugly, Guigsy shrewdly mentioned Robin Friday's name.

'Bloody hell, boyo! How do you know about him?' they exclaimed. And we swapped names and numbers. Nineteen years down the line and the name Robin Friday still stops people in their tracks.

Robin Friday, the unknown footballer, was adored everywhere he went and then, in 1977, he disappeared from public view. He spent the next 13 years working intermittently with his twin brother Tony, still refusing to bow down to anyone. He went inside for impersonating a policeman and stripping people of their drugs.

He had the odd game here and there. He married and separated for a third time. He was in and out of hospital. And, then, without warning, one Christmas he was gone. His heart, it seemed, had given up. The coroner recorded an open verdict.

He was brought here to Ruislip Crematorium and hundreds of people came to pay their respects. Then they left Robin to the silence, his life now an intrinsic part of their memories, their hearts glad that he had touched them just as he touched all those lucky enough to see him play.

But a grave was always going to be too small to accommodate Robin Friday. The proof of that is the existence of this book.

In the writing of it both myself and Guigsy were struck by one indisputable fact: there was not one person that we spoke to who had a bad word to say about Robin. Sure, they may have disapproved of his lifestyle, his bawdy nature or his direct manner. But they all recognised his great human spirit, his generosity and concern for others. 'Robin?' they would say. 'He would give you his last penny.'

If any proof was needed, Tommy Youlden, a keep-fit fanatic and a key player in Reading's promotion year, makes for a marvellous example. During his spell at Reading, Tommy did little to hide his displeasure at Robin's lifestyle. But at Robin's funeral on 4 January 1991 he was there to pay his respects.

This book then is our way of paying respect. Appropriately, we started around the time of Euro 96. Our first port of call was

Graham Wray whose brilliant article had first brought Robin to our attention. It is he who contributed the chapter on Robin's sojourn in Cardiff and brought Robin into our lives. Enough said.

Through Graham we located Robin's twin brother Tony, who in turn led us to his parents, Alf and Sheila Friday. Their support and help, especially Tony's, was absolutely invaluable.

We spent an inordinate amount of hours at the *Reading Evening Post* going through every issue that pertained to Robin's stay at the club. All of the staff there were great but we must just single out Clive 'The Hound' Baskerville and Stewart 'Four Goals a Season' Turkington in these dispatches. The Hound's contacts and endless suggestions plus Mr Turkington's work in the darkroom helped our cause no end. Equally, their coverage of our book and in particular the adventures of Guigsy in Reading were always stimulating.

We were lucky to meet up with Robin's first child Nicola Friday on one of her brief UK visits. However, her resistance to tape-recorders meant that due to the nature of this book we had to leave her out through fear of misquoting her. No such problem with Lisa, Robin's second wife, who enthusiastically put us in touch with Arabella, the daughter she had by Robin, as well as with friends such as Syd Simmonds and, inadvertently, Rod Lewington.

For the all-important appreciation of Robin's skills we were fortunate to spend a fascinating afternoon with the ex-Reading manager Charlie Hurley. We also gained access to players such as Eamon Dunphy and John 'Minty' Murray. Reading FC fanatics such as Roger Titford, co-author of a fine book about their promotion season entitled *More Than a Job*, and historian David Downs provided great overviews of both Robin and Reading.

The fact that whoever we spoke to or approached were more than happy to put aside as much time as was needed to talk about

Robin says much more about that unique individual than we can.

In London, *GQ* editor James Brown must be thanked not only for his astute editorial suggestions but also for losing the £60 cheque I recently gave him. Big, big thanks also to Irvine Welsh for writing the foreword and remaining an inspirational character. May your search for the key to the house of love be as fruitful as your writing, sir.

As we sat down to write this book, two people must be publicly saluted for their love and help with this project. They are Ruth, Guigsy's wife, who endured her husband's long absences in a smoke-filled room with unbelievable grace, endless pots of coffee and top scran, and Tony French, who helped out with the typing and supplied some very welcome suggestions. None of which we took.

Finally, let me just explain the book's structure. Guigsy and I were unfortunate enough never to have met Robin or seen him play, so it quickly became apparent as we sat down with the wonderful array of characters you are about to meet that it was only through their memories and voices, backed up by extracts from the *Reading Evening Post*, that the real Robin would emerge. We start then in a Britain from a long, long time ago and, as we do, both Guigsy and I would like to extend a very real thanks to all those who spoke to us.

Paolo Hewitt
August 1997

Friday's Child –
Running Wild

SHEILA FRIDAY, MOTHER: We've been married for 45 years now. I came from Acton Green and Alf came from South Acton. We met at the Boathouse in Kew. Do you remember it?

ALF FRIDAY, FATHER: It's long gone now. We couldn't go far when we were young. We used to go to the Empire and it would cost you two bob to go in the gods. Then we'd go down to Acton afterwards and have a sandwich. It was better then. All people think about is money now because you've got to have money. It was a lot more simple then.

SHEILA FRIDAY: We met when we were about 17 and got married when we were 20 in St Peter's Church in St Albans Avenue. We lived with my mum first. Robin and Tony were born a year later on 27 July 1952. Robin was first because he was the biggest. He was 7lb 9oz and Tony was 6lb 1oz. We were still living with my mum at number 21 Graham Road, because you couldn't get a place in them days.

ALF FRIDAY: We all lived there. Her brother lived there, her mum and gran.

TONY FRIDAY, BROTHER: Robin and I were born in Hammersmith and the difference in time between us was three minutes. He had two inches on every minute on me because he was about 6ft 2in. You could see we were twins. I mean, people who knew us close could always tell. Certain traits, certain mannerisms.

SHEILA FRIDAY: My dad played football. He played at Brentford one time and he played for Corinthian Casuals. He's only been dead two years. He was 93 when he died. His name was Frederick Riding. Anyway, when the children were about two, we moved to a prefab in Acton Green – 3 Gladstone Road – and we stayed there for about seven or eight years. The boys went to Rothchild Infant School and from there they went to Farraday School. Tony stayed on until he was 16.

ALF FRIDAY: At that time I was working on the laundry, driving, and I had other jobs in between. I use to have loads of jobs in those days.

SHEILA FRIDAY: They were good kids. Robin was actually very shy – he used to hide behind you. When they were young they would say to me, 'Mum, if we ever saw you talking to another man we wouldn't talk to you ever again.'

ALF FRIDAY: But they wasn't nasty to one another, ever. They never argued. They were never jealous of one another, like kids now. Tony was a little more upfront.

SHEILA FRIDAY: They never went outside in the garden – only with Alf. That changed when we moved to South Acton and the estate. It changed when Robin went to Farraday School.

ALF FRIDAY: You lose contact with them. When you live three floors up, once they go out they've sort of gone. In the prefabs you could watch them running around the garden – keep an eye on them. The prefab was beautiful. Two bedrooms, a kitchen, sitting-room, separate bathrooms. I'd like one now.

SHEILA FRIDAY: We had to move out because the prefab was sinking. So they moved us to this estate, 40 Cain House.

ALF FRIDAY: It was all right when we moved in, but you wouldn't want to go there now. We had a maisonette with two tower blocks behind us.

TONY FRIDAY: My mum's dad played for Brentford before the war. Pre-war they were a good side, Brentford. I don't know exactly how many games he played – he might only have been a combination league player because they all had big squads then. They don't do it now because of the money side of things. My dad played but he was just a park player. He enjoyed his football but he never played at a higher level. He worked as a driver on the laundry. Where we lived in South Acton it was called Soap Sud Island because there were so many laundries there.

ALF FRIDAY: I played football with them when they were four.

SHEILA FRIDAY: Every day he would take them to the park to play. He took them to Brentford when they were two years old to watch the team play.

ALF FRIDAY: It was a shit game an' all.

SHEILA FRIDAY: Every day he would finish at four on the laundry and then he'd take them to South Fields Park.

ALF FRIDAY: No, I'd take them to Acton Green. Robin used to go in goal – he used to be brilliant in goal. He was only about five and he used to swing himself all over the place. I used to pump that ball up really hard. That was when valve balls first came out, and they did away with those laced-up ones.

SHEILA FRIDAY: What about the first football kit we gave them that Christmas?

ALF FRIDAY: That was an Everton outfit, wasn't it?

SHEILA FRIDAY: We put their presents at the end of the bed and when we got up in the morning and they were fast asleep in bed with the whole kit on: boots, shorts and the top.

ALF FRIDAY: They only supported Everton when they were little because they *were* the team then. Alec Young and that mob – big Brian Labone. Lovely little side. They supported Brentford after that.

TONY FRIDAY: When we lived in the prefab there was a park at the end of the road and our old man would have us over there every night. I can always remember him buying us a leather football one Christmas, a lovely one. Not like the right old leather ones with the laces that would do your head in. We used to be forever playing football, and I would say that anything achieved by Robin really is a big tribute to my dad. He was always there and in later years when Robin was playing the old man was at every game. He'd travel up north when Robin played for Reading and then when he went to Cardiff my dad would go there to see him.

ALF FRIDAY: They used to play about in the prefabs. You know Brentford? Georgie Francis and Jimmy Towers? I don't know if you've ever heard of them but they used to play for Brentford and they used to call George – what was it? Checker. He came from

South Acton – all these players came from South Acton: Alan Devonshire, David Cox, Warren Neil. But Georgie, he had the nickname Checker, and either Tony or Robin, when they had a kickabout, one of them would say 'I'll be George' and the other one would say 'I'll be Checker'. I'd be going, 'you can't both be him'.

SHEILA FRIDAY: Great that was. They would play with grown men then.

ALF FRIDAY: Funnily enough, when they were over at the junior school, Tony got into the team first. Tony was a fair little player and Robin started when he was about ten, just before they left Rothchild. At 11 they were both in a team at Farraday and then they went on from there into the district side. Robin would get hold of an orange, flick it up onto his neck, and roll it down. He was really skilful with his juggling.

SHEILA FRIDAY: You know like that boy in the advert on the telly? Well, Robin could do all that.

TONY FRIDAY: He liked Bestie, obviously. He liked Pele and he liked Peter Osgood, but when he was younger Greavsie was the boy for him because he was scoring all the goals.

SHEILA FRIDAY: Did you know he used to box?

TONY FRIDAY: Boxing, tennis.

ALF FRIDAY: And cricket, and he was a good bowler – a fucking good bowler. I'll tell you, he was a bit tasty. I reckon he could have made it as a bowler. When he was 13 he used to bowl them down and I couldn't see them. He had the height.

TONY FRIDAY: I was always in the top class and he was in the second-to-bottom. He wasn't a dope, he just wasn't interested. He was always bunking off, having birds around the park.

SHEILA FRIDAY: He was clever, Tony. Every time we went up to the school – when they want the parents to go up – the teachers used to always say to my husband: 'All I can say is that all your boys ever talk about is football.' When Tony played for the school they used to put a notice up on the board: 'And our only supporter, Mr Friday . . .' He always went to their school games, didn't you, Alf?

TONY FRIDAY: I was in the football team at primary school before Robin, believe it or not. I played midfield. A schemer, that's what I was. Put a ball inside the back four. I was a fair player as it happens. I went to most of the clubs that Robin was at in the Isthmian league. But, obviously, if you were with someone like him who's going and getting hat-tricks, you're sort of over-shadowed.

ALF FRIDAY: Robin could be the nicest boy you've ever met in your life. I was on the post and I used to get up at half-past four and sometimes he would come in and say, 'You don't have to go to work today, do you, Dad?' Then he used to watch me out of the window as I went to work. I used to look back and see him watching me. That's what he was like.

TONY FRIDAY: We played for the school on a Saturday morning, a youth side in the afternoon and maybe a pub side on the Sunday. I remember when we played four games of a weekend when we were younger. We started playing with men when we were 14. We played for the Acton British Legion Reserves. And actually one day my dad played as well so there was me and Robin and me old man playing in the same side. We were playing with men from about 14 or 15 onwards, which is how you improve as a player.

★ ★ ★

ALF FRIDAY: He liked a bit of heavy metal. He loved Janis Joplin and I can't stand her.

SHEILA FRIDAY: He used to go to the Roundhouse [a north London music venue]. He saw everyone there. They used to come on the TV and he'd say, 'I seen them at the Roundhouse.' All them singers he used to see. He'd go on a Sunday afternoon.

TONY FRIDAY: He liked Desmond Dekker and he loved Frankie Miller.

SHEILA FRIDAY: He used to go to the dances at the Hayes Football Club. They used to lay on the dances there. They cleared the floor with their dancing. They were doing the funky chicken, mucking about, and Robin did it so good they cleared the floor to watch him.

TONY FRIDAY: I watched a TV programme on Saturday night, *The Rock'n'Roll Years*, and he loved the old Stax records. Otis, Sam and Dave, and all of them. But he also liked Desmond Dekker and all that ska music. I think my mum's still got all of his old records – and he had loads. But then he went from that to his favourite artist of all time – Janis Joplin. He loved Janis Joplin. Funnily enough, his life was a sort of a mirror of hers in a way.

★ ★ ★

TONY FRIDAY: We was always in the district side and although we was only a small borough compared to, say, South London or Islington, who had a huge range to pick from, we used to beat them. In our actual side there was Stevie Perryman, Robin, a guy named David Coxhill who played for Millwall, and there was another fellow, Peter Carey, who was at West Ham. There were four or five who went on to be pros. When we were in the under-12s, under-13s, under-14s, Robin actually played for the District in goal. He was a brilliant goalkeeper. He had no fear. He would have been even more successful as a goalie. But he obviously preferred banging them in at the other end.

ALF FRIDAY: When did he go to that school of excellence at Crystal Palace? He and Carey went there.

TONY FRIDAY: He was about 12 or 13 when he was selected from the borough to go to Crystal Palace – not Crystal Palace Football Club, but the Crystal Palace sports club which used to be there – probably still is. They had a proper coaching thing. Who was that bloke doing it? I remember he said something to Robin, didn't he? Who was it now, a proper coach?

ALF FRIDAY: Was it that old bloke out of Chelsea? Harry Medhurst, that's him, he liked Robin. See, you can't push someone into something like football. You obviously think they're good because you are their parents but you also know their limitations. I wrote to Chelsea for him for a trial when he was about 13 and he got in.

SHEILA FRIDAY: He went to Wembley with them for the FA Cup final.

ALF FRIDAY: May 1967. Chelsea lost 2–1 to Spurs.

SHEILA FRIDAY: He used to go to that restaurant, Dino's. They used to give him a voucher to go into Dino's and get something to eat.

ALF FRIDAY: He was only there for about a year. Then they have a clear out if they don't fancy you. Tommy Docherty was the manager then.

SHEILA FRIDAY: I remember going in one morning to wake him up and he said, 'Mum, I was just dreaming I was on the Wembley pitch.'

ALF FRIDAY: He never ever said he was going to be a pro. It wasn't his scene, really. When he left Chelsea he just played park football.

TONY FRIDAY: When he was 13 or 14 he had a season training down the [Queen's Park] Rangers. The guy who was in charge of the youth team was called Dennis Healey. Alex Stock was the manager then and Robin used to go training there on Tuesdays and Thursdays. Robin was picked for the District side and then he went on to Chelsea. He was there for quite a while. The reason he never made it at them clubs was because he was always very much his own player. He wouldn't play the easy ball, he would always try something. They try to instil things in players and that's what is wrong with our football.

TONY FRIDAY: We had different mates, which was good. We weren't always with each other. Because he was always a lot bigger than me, Robin was out and about before me, starting with the birds and what have you. He was about 15 when he started popping a few pills first of all. That was one thing I never got into.

ALF FRIDAY: That's something you cannot control. A person is going to do what they are going to do. When someone is grown up you cannot tell them what to do. See, the difference with me is that with my dad dying so young I never had anyone to boss me about so I can't set a precedent. I don't think I ever came heavy with them. Obviously I would eff and blind at them, and if they did things wrong, then I'd say, 'Well, you ain't doing yourself no good'. But I can't sit in judgement on other people. You can't run someone else's life. You can't stop them.

TONY FRIDAY: It was sporadic. In them days when you were 15 or 16 everyone started with Blues [speed pills] but then they did a bit of methadone and that was skin-popping. Robin wasn't one for half measures . . . But he wouldn't be dependent on it, so to speak. Sometimes you'd hear stories that he'd been doing it before a game. But that's all bollocks.

ALF FRIDAY: Robin left school at 15. He was brilliant at drawing and he just stopped doing it – I couldn't make it out. He could draw lifelike. He used to draw Andy Capp. Sheila's dad was round one day and said, 'He ain't done that, he's copied that, traced it'. I said, 'He ain't, he's drawn it'. Then Robin just suddenly stopped.

TONY FRIDAY: We had a side called South Acton and the other team we played for was a team called St Cuthbert's. The old guy who used to run them was called Harry Fountain. He was a right lad, him, and he loved Robin because he reminded him of the players of olden times. He was an old bricklayer and he must have been 70 then but he would still give you a right-hander. I could always remember one game when we played this team from the Spartan League which was a more senior league than ours. We beat them 6–0 and Robin got all six goals. Harry ran on the pitch and kissed him. It was the only time he'd ever shown a bit of emotion in his life.

* * *

TONY FRIDAY: When he first left school he went into a plastering firm to learn the business but he never was into work.

SHEILA FRIDAY: My husband's grandfather was a plasterer. I don't know where Robin got it from because he never knew his grandfather, but Robin wanted to do plastering. When he left school I took him to a place in Ealing, it was a real high-class place with high ceilings and he got the job. But he left it after two months. He did loads of different jobs. He worked at Ferris's, worked as a van boy for a grocery firm. He used to go and deliver from the warehouse to the shops.

ALF FRIDAY: He said to me one Saturday, 'Here, Dad, come up and give me a hand with this window cleaning', cos I never used to work Saturdays. He was going up that ladder like the clappers. He was shouting to me, 'Don't stand over them, just give them a wiz'. He didn't have a barrow, he used to carry the ladder. Imagine it. He was a lad, Robin. You had to laugh at him – he didn't care.

SHEILA FRIDAY: And he liked the asphalting, didn't he?

ALF FRIDAY: He met a geezer at Walthamstow Avenue and he took him on. It wasn't the roads, it was roofs.

TONY FRIDAY: He went to borstal when he was 16, Robin. Strangely enough, that helped him a bit. He had plenty of convictions already but the one which got him borstal was a silly bit of stealing – a car radio or something. He got a DC first, a detention centre, but he got out of that because he had asthma. But about three months later he was nicked for something else and he got borstal. That was in Feltham. The one he actually went to was the one where blokes who had drug problems go to. He did something like 14 months, but while he was there they had a football side and they started winning everything because Robin was so brilliant. He got strong when he was there. He filled out more. He was always tall but skinny, but he filled right out because he was eating three meals a day. It did him good, to be honest with you. He even got selected for the league side while he was there and they let him play. An escort came out with him and he played for a representative side when he was only 16 – and it was men's teams. Right at the end of your borstal term, you go to a finishing one for the last six weeks. The PTI there, Hinchmore Wood I think it was, saw Robin playing. He got onto Reading and said, 'I've got this player', and Robin used to go and play for Reading Juniors in the South-east Counties League. Then he came home and he and Maxine got their flat together in South Acton.

★ ★ ★

ALF FRIDAY: He was always nice to coloureds. Always. He got on really well with them – which is saying something, because mostly the guys round South Acton wanted them all back home, like. He got on with them great.

SHEILA FRIDAY: Robin was 17 when he married Maxine. She had a flat in Larden Road. We were against it but she had the baby.

ALF FRIDAY: But it wasn't only that. I suppose he wanted to get away.

SHEILA FRIDAY: Then they got married. I went to the wedding. Alf didn't go. It was at the Acton town hall. Then he came back home and met another girl – I can't remember her name. She was nice. He always went with girls who were a bit classy. Then he went back to Maxine.

ROD LEWINGTON, FRIEND: In those days a black guy might have gone with a white woman but you never saw a white guy with a black woman. It was unheard of. Robin was the only one I know who did it. Once again, unique.

TONY FRIDAY: Maxine lived in Acton as well. There was a place we all used to go to in Acton, the White Hart, and that's where Robin met her. It was like a pub with a dance hall on the side, and that was the first place everyone went. She had her own flat – there was some trouble with her mum – and he used to go and stay there. Which is when she got pregnant with Nicola. Maxine was a good sort. She always mixed with our circle of friends. In them days that was not the done thing. He had a ruck one night when he was playing at Hayes. There was a little mob in there. None of us was there. They had a do after a game one night and he took Maxine. Someone said something and then there was a big ruck. He had a fight with a couple of people. In them days he would rebel, he would never go with the norm.

TONY FRIDAY: A friend of ours was playing at Walthamstow Avenue and he took Robin down there. They saw he was a bit tasty so Robin started training down there. They were a good old side, Walthamstow – bit of tradition there, amateur cup-winners, that sort of thing. Robin got in the side and they were in the Isthmian League and from there on he started scoring goals. Then they played Hayes and I think they beat them and the manager tapped him up. He knew Walthamstow was a long way to go and he knew that Robin was a local boy – Acton isn't that far from Hayes – and Walthamstow were never good payers. Robin was on a tenner at Walthamstow and when he went to Hayes I think he got 30 quid a week. But while he was at Walthamstow there were a lot of guys from the East End there and they worked on the asphalt. So they got Robin a job on the asphalt, too.

SHEILA FRIDAY: That was where he had that terrible accident. He was 20 when he had that accident. I picked that call up from the police. They rang my office and said he was in St Thomas's Hospital in London behind the Houses of Parliament. We bowled up there but they wouldn't let us see him. He was in theatre for six hours. He was 21 at the end of that week and we had bought him new boots. We didn't know whether to give them to him or not – but he got over that. He was ever so strong, wasn't he?

ALF FRIDAY: Unbelievable. It wasn't that long before he was back down at Hayes playing. Unbelievably strong.

TONY FRIDAY: He was on the scaffold and the hoist rope got stuck. He tried to jump on the scaffold to free this hoist rope and he went straight down and this spike went up his arse. He pulled himself off, which is a feat and a half in itself, really. He was strong. Luckily enough it was at Lambeth and it was right near St Thomas's Hospital. He was in the operating theatre for hours.

TONY FRIDAY: Hayes played Bristol Rovers in the first round of the cup. And it was at Hayes and they beat Rovers. Robin played great but he didn't get the goal – a geezer named Bobby Hat scored – but it was really a good game and Bristol Rovers were a good side. As I say, they beat them 1–0 and the champagne was flowing. They played Reading away in the next round, and they drew 0–0. Robin had a great game that day. They pulled them back to Hayes for the replay but Reading beat them 1–0. Hayes were a bit unlucky. They had a few chances but they didn't stick them away. But obviously, from that day on, the Reading manager Charlie Hurley thought, 'Hold up. I fancy this geezer.'

1974: By Royal Appointment – The King of Reading

ROGER TITFORD, AUTHOR: Charlie Hurley was a 'get out of the trenches and at them' kind of manager. Big strong boys, no fairies – pretty unsophisticated, really. It was his first job in management and his last. He wasn't against playing attractive football but, frankly, I think he was a bit nervous of management. I think the best thing he did as a manager was to find Robin, dare to play him and dare to keep him happy in the team. As far as I know, Friday was never thrown out of the team for disciplinary reasons. I don't think he was ever dropped. Whether Charlie had any control of his off-the-pitch activities, well, I shouldn't think he did. As long as Robin was doing it for him on the pitch, Charlie couldn't complain.

ALF FRIDAY: Charlie Hurley was a great guy. I liked Charlie a lot.

DAVID DOWNS, READING FC HISTORIAN: The first time I saw Robin play was at Hayes when they played Reading in the FA Cup in 1973. Robin played at Reading and in the replay at Hayes. What was interesting about the replay was that he fouled Reading's keeper, Steve Death, and caused him to hobble around for so long that the ref actually booked Steve for time-wasting. That was the only time Steve Death was booked in a 12-year career with Reading.

CHARLIE HURLEY, READING MANAGER: I was desperate for a striker and I used to go to Hayes a lot. They were in the Isthmian League, a very good league in fact. When I look back, I should have got more players from there. I knew Robin's reputation. I had done my research. I actually went to the matches at Hayes and I was going up to a lot of people in the crowd saying, 'Who's this kid playing number nine? Seems a bit of a nutter to me.' The fans would respond: 'We don't worry about that as long as he does it for us on the park.' I found out that he had been in borstal, maybe the nick, I don't know. When you're in the Fourth Division you look at players *on* the pitch, not *off* it, because you can't have it all.

After that cup game I watched Robin for a while and then I signed him. I got him for 750 quid! I signed him as an amateur to play in the reserves. The first match he played in was a midweek game and it was twenty past seven, which is when you should have the team list in with the referee. And in comes this guy covered in brick dust, filthy boots – a real sight. He looked a bit useful so there weren't too many of them in the dressing-room who were going to call him scruffy. He goes out onto the pitch and instantly you can see his talent, instantly the best player I had in the reserves. His positional play wasn't all that great, but on the ball he was absolutely tremendous. And his vision was marvellous. I thought, 'I've got to have a go at this, bugger it.' After the game I asked him about the team. He said, 'You've got a lot of poofs out there, boss!' And he was absolutely right. I agreed with him but beggars can't be choosers. I wanted to sign him immediately.

MAURICE EVANS, READING TRAINER: Robin lived in Acton and Charlie told me he went to sign him at his flat. All the family were there and Robin said, 'Sit down on the settee.' Charlie sat down and the arm fell off the settee.

Reading Evening Post
. . . Amateur striker Robin Friday has played three games in the reserves . . .

DAVID DOWNS, READING FC HISTORIAN: In his very first training session they were playing a six-a-side game and Robin went round trying to kick as many of the established Reading players as he could. He must have put two or three out of this game. Hurley had to call him off and say, 'Robin, slow down a minute. Let's talk about what you're doing here before you finish off the rest of the team.'

CHARLIE HURLEY: He trained like he played. I sent him off a few times from training sessions for kicking his own team-mates in five-a-side games (which was always his favourite game). Robin would play five-a-side like he would play on a Saturday. He had no other way of playing.

Reading Evening Post, 21 January 1974
. . . Reading have won twice in their last 14 games . . .

CHARLIE HURLEY: I realised early on that there was no way you were going to get him to wear a collar and tie. I remember when I actually signed him, I said to him, 'You've got to wear a jacket.' He said, 'I don't have any jackets.' So I brought this blazer in for him. He was effing and blinding when he put it on but I told him that if he wanted to sign, he had to wear it. We did a quick photograph and then he took it off straightaway. He was a real jeans man so I tried to get him to wear smart jeans as opposed to working jeans.

Reading Evening Post, 24 January 1974
. . . Hayes striker Robin Friday has signed Football League forms for Reading and may make his début in Sunday's forthcoming game at

Northampton although Hurley wanted to give him a longer run in the reserves . . . Friday played for Hayes against Reading in the second round of the FA Cup. He has not scored in his recent outings for the reserves but came within inches of doing so in all three games . . .

CHARLIE HURLEY: We started having Sunday football matches. On the Thursday I had Robin in the office and said, 'I am thinking of giving you a game on Sunday against Northampton.' 'Oh, boss,' he said, 'look, I'll go home, I won't drink, I won't fight.'

'Don't go crazy,' I said, 'I don't mind you lying but not three times.'

27 January 1974
Reading 3 Northampton 3

Reading Evening Post, 30 January 1974
Robin Friday, the amateur who made such an outstanding début for Reading against Northampton last weekend, almost lost his life in an accident at work last year. Star striker Friday told me at his home in South Acton last night, 'I fell on a big spike which went through my backside into my stomach and just missed a lung. The doctors told me that I was a fraction of an inch away from death.' After three months in hospital Friday regained fitness shortly before he played for Hayes against Reading in the FA Cup when Elm Park boss Charlie Hurley first saw him in action. Now Hurley must decide whether to offer a professional contract to his new find. If and when he does, the situation will present Robin Friday with a real problem, for to come to Reading he will have to take a pay cut of about half his present wage as an asphalter.

He said, 'I want to be a pro and I want to be one with Reading, but with a wife and child I've got to consider the money situation. At the moment Hayes want me to continue playing for them but I can't turn out for them on Saturdays when Reading are playing on

Sundays. I don't want to let the Hayes lads down so I was substitute last Saturday and fortunately they didn't need me. I think they want me to be substitute again this Saturday but obviously this situation can't continue. As it happens, it was only because I had a bad illness a couple of months ago that I'm playing for Reading. Watford asked me to play for their reserve team and I would probably be there now if I hadn't had this bug in my stomach.'

Friday, in fact, is now in his second spell with Reading. Five seasons ago he played for their South-east Counties League side as a 16-year-old. After three games, Jack Mansell didn't pick him again but Friday is determined to make it this time. He said, 'I've always had a lot of confidence and I know I can do well for Reading. It would have been really great if I had scored in the last minute against Northampton – I thought the shot was going in. I was really shattered in the last minute but that's not surprising when you consider that I only train two nights a week. I know I won't let Reading down, I always give 100 per cent and I always put myself about.'

Down at Elm Park, Hurley is understandably playing it a bit cagey. 'I shall have to take a good look at him over three or four games. One swallow doesn't make a summer.'

Reading Evening Post, 1 February 1974
Reading have not won away for four months and Hurley will be hoping that the extra strength up front added by the introduction of amateur Robin Friday will continue to produce goals to end this barren spell.

ROD LEWINGTON, FRIEND: I first met Robin in 1973. He was highly unusual to say the least. A very genuine guy. Everybody he met seemed to take a liking to him and he would talk to anyone. He was always up for the crack. Terrific sense of humour and the ability to laugh at himself.

Reading Evening Post, 3 February 1974

Barnsley 3 Reading 2

. . . Reading found themselves two goals down at half-time . . . drastic action was clearly needed . . . Les Chapell went up at the near post and although he completely missed his header, he managed to deceive the Barnsley goalkeeper and Robin Friday nipped in at the far post to nod home his first league goal. Typical of his confidence was his comment about the goal he scored. 'I was thinking of chesting it down and backheeling it in but I thought I'd better not muck about.' He is now deciding whether to move down to Reading from his home in South Acton.

CHARLIE HURLEY: We were playing at Barnsley and we're losing 2–0. Half-time comes and I went potty. I changed the team slightly and we got to 2–2. Then they sent on a substitute and I thought, 'This is strange. They're playing at home and they've sent on a defender as a sub.' Normally you would put an attacker on to try and win the match. After the game – we lost 3–2 – Robin said, 'Hey, boss, that sub they sent on – he was sent on to ask me if I wanted to sign for Barnsley.'

Reading Evening Post, 6 February 1974

Robin Friday, Reading's new striker sensation, signed a professional contract for the club today. After three games as an amateur, Friday will make his home début as a pro in the club's next Fourth Division game against Exeter City on Sunday. Friday gave up his job as an asphalter yesterday and decided to become a pro after talks in the afternoon with manager Charlie Hurley. The signing of Friday gives the club an unprecedented 21 professionals. Hurley said, 'I know we're way over the limit now but what can you do when you have a player like Robin Friday? We had to make an exception for him.'

TONY FRIDAY: You know how people are always saying that Robin didn't give two fucks? Well, he was the first to get out of the estate. Now we're all out of it but he actually bought a house when he got a chunk of money for signing to Reading. He was still with Maxine then, but when he was playing for Reading, what I think happened is that a lot of the time after training or games they would go out and have a giggle – and that's when the cracks started to appear in their marriage.

Reading Evening Post, 9 February 1974
Charlie Hurley writes: 'It seems a long while since we played at Elm Park having scored five goals in our last two away games compared to one in the previous six games. We hope you're all raring to find out how we all did it. Someone who has played no small part in the goal-scoring spree is Robin Friday, the amateur I signed from Hayes last Wednesday. He is 6ft tall, 21 years old, frightened of no one and very skilful, a player you supporters will want to see in his first Fourth Division game . . . So don't forget, come and see Friday on Sunday. Excuse the pun, I couldn't resist it.'

CHARLIE HURLEY: In the lower divisions, in fact the lower down you are in the Football League, you find you have to shut not just one eye, but you have to half shut the other one too. The question you have to ask is: does he ever let you down on the pitch?

Reading Evening Post, 10 February 1974
Reading 4 Exeter 1
. . . Those who braved the downpour were rewarded by some excellent entertainment. They also saw a performance by Reading's newest professional, Robin Friday, which was not short of sheer magic . . . In only his third league game, Friday showed such ability and guts, such enthusiasm and willingness to take on opponents, that the main thing worrying fans afterwards was how long we can

keep him? . . . The real excitement was packed into the last quarter of an hour . . . First Exeter skipper Mike Balson was booked for a foul on Friday and then the referee made an absolutely dumbfounded decision by refusing to award a penalty when Friday was brought down . . . But on this occasion the plot had a new twist . . . When, with ten minutes left, Reading looked close to throwing away the match they had almost always dominated, Robin Friday conjured two glorious goals in the space of three minutes . . . Wide to the left of goal, Friday went past four challenges before cracking the ball from 18 yards low into the far corner of the net . . . To a man the fans in the stands rose to Friday to salute what they thought was a dream ending to his début . . . But he wasn't finished yet . . . Substitute Dick Habbin came on for the towering Wagstaff and immediately produced an accurate centre to the near post where Friday had again found space to stoop low and flick home a delicate header . . . Fans are no doubt wondering where Reading would be in the table now if they had had the services of Robin Friday and Tommy Youlden all season.

Reading Evening Post, 12 February 1974
Robin Friday says: 'Charlie Hurley has given me my chance and I mean to take it. I always knew I was good enough for league football but no one was willing to give me the opportunity before. Now that Mr Hurley has given it to me, I will give them nothing but 100 per cent all the time. I felt just great after those two goals. I could tell the crowd loved them and that was half the battle, keeping the fans happy. I took a lot of stick. I expect to, the way I play. The only way to answer back when you are being kicked all over the place is to pop in a couple of goals. I was sick when the ref didn't give us a penalty when I was tripped, but what can you say about that? Ridiculous. I'm really enjoying playing with lads who appreciate it when you hold the ball – I've got a great understanding with Percy Freeman. Some sides I've played in thought I was greedy, but I know that if I hold the ball I can score a lot of goals.'

DAVID DOWNS: Robin would never ever wear shinpads either in training or when playing. He would go out like a Sunday League player and however badly he was fouled – and he did get some terrible kickings and beatings – he would just get on and carry on. While the more experienced players would get the physio on, Robin would just get up and start again.

Reading Evening Post, 16 February 1974

. . . New boy Robin Friday has been struggling all week to shake off the effects of the battering he received in the Exeter game, a calf injury being the main problem.

Reading Evening Post, 17 February 1974

Lincoln 0 Reading 2

. . . Not only were Reading without the injured Tommy Youlden, Stewart Henderson and Dennis Butler, but they also had Robin Friday semi-crippled almost from the first minute when Ellis crudely hacked Friday to the ground . . . At least half a dozen more times Reading's new star had his legs kicked from under him, and at one stage, after Cooper had been booked in the 35th minute, Friday had to come off for five minutes . . . But in the end his skill triumphed over Lincoln's butchery . . . Although he was literally on his knees at the final whistle, he had the satisfaction of making both goals . . . Friday went down the right, beat the right-back and crossed perfectly from the goal-line for Freeman to shoot home . . .

Reading had to wait 11 minutes from the end for the goal which put the result beyond doubt . . . Again it started with Friday who appeared to have no hope of creating anything when he got the ball near the left-hand corner flag with his back to goal and with two men on his back . . . It took a flash of his own inimitable genius to wriggle past three men and get the ball deep into the box where Les Chapell touched it back for Barry Wagstaff to slam it home.

CHARLIE HURLEY: First thing in the game, most centre-halves used to go in hard on the tackle and see how Robin would react. He would get kicked to ribbons out there and he never ever complained. An awful amount of centre-forwards would be looking over their shoulders for the rest of the match. Robin would be looking to get back in there. One time this fellow was going to tackle a free-kick. He ran by Robin and Robin grabbed him by the balls. The ref didn't know what to do. That was Robin.

★ ★ ★

ROD LEWINGTON: He drank lager. There was a very strong lager at the time called Colt 45 which is what he drank. I never saw him drink spirits.

ALF FRIDAY: He could drink Southern Comfort all night long.

SHEILA FRIDAY: And he wouldn't be drunk.

ROD LEWINGTON: I remember one night Robin ended up in The Crown in Caversham and he was leaping from table to table. Finally, the landlord told him he was barred, by which time Robin was standing on the bar. It was complete mayhem.

★ ★ ★

Reading Evening Post, 21 February 1974
George Best has been charged with stealing jewellery from Miss Marjorie Wallace's flat.

Reading Evening Post, 24 February 1974
Reading 5 Doncaster 0

. . . Happy days are here again at Elm Park. The long queues of fans outside the ground before yesterday's game were rewarded with Reading's best win for 17 months . . . Reading's third win on the trot puts them up to seventh place and cuts the gap between them and fourth-placed Bury to just four points . . . The team that has been transformed by Robin Friday has now scored a remarkable 16 goals in five games and the highlight of this joyous afternoon was a goal by Friday that was worth anyone's admission money on its own . . . First, Doncaster's defence was in total disarray when Friday beat two men inside the box and turned the ball back for Percy Freeman whose wild shot was flashing harmlessly wide until Les Chapell sent a header rocketing into the goal . . .

If this goal was a gem, the one that followed in the 17th minute was strictly 24 carat . . . The golden goal move started with Barry Wagstaff sending Friday clear of the defence . . . Friday kept his cool and put in a low shot to the far post from 15 yards. I was right behind the line of the shot and it appeared at first to be missing the post with a couple of yards to spare. But Friday had magically coaxed the ball with his boot and at the last possible second it literally changed course, bending in an amazing arc to clip the inside of the post and roll home.

DAVID DOWNS: Robin got the ball about 25 yards out from goal at quite a sharp angle and he did something which I have never seen any Reading player do before or since. He hit the ball on the outside of the foot and swerved it so that it actually curved right round the goalie and into the far corner of the net. I was lucky enough to be in line with the shot when it went in and you could see the amount of skill and effort that went into that particular goal. He stayed in the side after that right through to the end of the season.

★ ★ ★

CHARLIE HURLEY: When you're pigeon-toed, as Robin was, when you hit a ball there will always be spin on it.

Reading Evening Post, 25 February 1974
. . . Reading's visit to Swansea on Sunday will be the longest trip for any club this weekend. However, following their three wins on the trot, three coachloads of fans have already booked up to make the trip.

Reading Evening Post, 3 March 1974
Swansea 2 Reading 1
. . . Bryan Carnaby was the first man to be cautioned for a late tackle on Lulley and Robin Friday followed him into the book for abusive language when pointing out that Wynn Edwards had opened up a deep cut over his eye . . . Besides his booking, Friday was a big disappointment.

Reading Evening Post, 11 March 1974
Reading 2 Workington 0
. . . Robin Friday was the main inspiration with a series of clever ideas that kept the entertainment level high.

Reading Evening Post, 16 March 1974
Mansfield 1 Reading 1
. . . Only six minutes had passed when Barry Wagstaff fired in what looked like a perfect goal. At any rate even the Mansfield players looked surprised when it was disallowed – apparently for offside against Robin Friday . . . That was the one black mark against Friday in an otherwise absolutely outstanding game. Time and again he beat two or three defenders and his ability to hold on to the ball and take it deep inside the Mansfield territory was a chief factor in Reading's supremacy . . . He got his reward in the end when he set up the equaliser but in the main was kept at bay by a series of disgraceful

fouls . . . Mansfield's Terry Eccles became the fourth player to be booked in eight games for fouling Robin Friday . . . It seems that Fourth Division players have given up trying to get the ball off him and are having more success with getting him off the ball. It is an accepted fact at this level that if a player is prepared to hold on to the ball he stands a great chance of being butchered.

DAVID DOWNS: He was an out-and-out centre-forward but, to be fair to Robin, when the team was struggling, he would do his share of tackling back and helping the defence. But his style of play was really quite bizarre. It was more or less Robin standing in the middle and saying, 'Give me the ball and I'll see what I can do with it.' People would pass the ball to him and he would turn, take players on and then either take a shot at goal himself or take it out wide and cross the ball and look for someone else to knock it in.

CHARLIE HURLEY: He had a brilliant sliding tackle for a centre-forward. He would slide, get the ball and bring it all up in one movement. It was brilliant how he did it.

Reading Evening Post, 20 March 1974
Reading I Barnsley 0
. . . Robin Friday, again the tormentor of a bemused defence, earned a free-kick just outside the area after 36 minutes . . . Barry Wagstaff strode up to take it but a poor free-kick left Friday stranded until the ball ricocheted to the unmarked Bruce Stuckey, who made no mistake . . . Friday came into his own when, following some brilliant work from Wagstaff, the skilful striker was just wide . . . Friday then showed superb footwork but his shot was blocked . . . The Barnsley winger Butler was booked for tripping up Friday . . . Reading are now in fifth place, having played 35 games gaining 39 points.

Reading Evening Post, 24 March 1974
Reading 0 Bradford 0
Charlie Hurley said: 'I would be more worried if we had been playing like this a lot but the general run of things over the last half a dozen games is that we have been playing well. It was just one of those days.'

Reading Evening Post, 27 March 1974
Crewe 2 Reading 1
 . . . Charlie Hurley has ordered extra training for his players. 'I do know that there were nine fouls on Friday, 17 corners to Crewe and five to Reading, which gives you a pretty accurate picture of what occurred in what little play there was.'

CHARLIE HURLEY: If we played well and got beaten that was one thing; but if we played badly and hadn't made the effort, I'd say, 'Right, you're coming in on Sunday.' No one likes work on Sundays. I'd say, 'I don't want to come in,' and Robin would shout out from the back, 'Well, don't bloody well come in.'

Reading Evening Post, 3 April 1974
Northampton 2 Reading 1
 . . . In the last minute Northampton's goalkeeper proved there was no justice in the world when he fingertipped a shot away from Friday after a brave solo run. The ball crept along the line but stayed out.

★ ★ ★

SHEILA FRIDAY: He was always with the fashions.

ALF FRIDAY: He never ever dressed like other people.

SHEILA FRIDAY: One day he came in with a satin suit and a lizardskin shirt. He always used to wear them.

ALF FRIDAY: Always in lizards.

SHEILA FRIDAY: He used to go to Kensington Market all the time. Even at Reading, he'd get Alf to take him before a game.

TONY FRIDAY: He was the first geezer, when he was about 16, to have an Afghan coat. When we were all walking around in Levi's with turn-ups, Sta-prest and Ben Sherman's and all that, he'd be in the hippy gear. Kensington Market was his place. He was a Kensington Market freak.

CHARLIE HURLEY: John Hulme was a good-looking lad – slicked-back hair, white polo-neck jumper and blazer – really immaculate. He used to stand next to Robin sometimes and I would say, 'You look like Bill and Ben – one a flower, one a straggly weed.' And Robin would look at John, shake his head and say, 'Yeah, I know what a weed he is!' But they got on well because it was a case of respect on the pitch and the greatest compliment you can get in any sport or any business is from your peers.

Reading Evening Post, 30 March 1974
Gillingham 0 Reading 1
. . . How can a team lose at Crewe, the 19th in the table, and win in their next game at Gillingham who are second? . . . Robin Friday, who miskicked the ball, succeeded in pushing it straight into the path of Les Chapell. Six yards out Chapell did what he was there for, playing it calmly wide of Gibson's left hand for the decider . . .

Thereafter Reading were never seriously in any danger of dropping a point. If anything, they were more likely to get a second, and Friday could perhaps have been expected to do better with his overhead shot from close in with one minute left . . . The young Gillingham fans rated Reading as one of the best teams they'd seen all season, and Reading's bewildered fans stood around asking, 'Why can't they do that every week?'

Reading Evening Post, 2 April 1974

. . . Barry Wagstaff out and a big doubt hanging over Robin Friday was the grim news from Elm Park before tomorrow's big promotion battle against Northampton. Friday was sent home from training on Monday with a sore throat and was in bed all day yesterday nursing a cold. He will take a fitness test shortly before kick-off, but if he doesn't feel well enough to play Percy Freeman will wear the number 9 shirt.

Reading Evening Post, 3 April 1974

Reading 1 Northampton 2

. . . Elm Park last night witnessed two of the most remarkable goals in its long history. They were both scored by Northampton midfield John Buchanan and they finally ended the impossible dream that Reading would be promoted to the Third Division. Reading could point out that they were without Barry Wagstaff for all of the game and without Robin Friday for the last half hour . . . Seven minutes before the break Friday, who spent all day Tuesday in bed with flu, pulled a shot wide with only the goalkeeper to beat when he really ought to have scored . . . It was admittedly a gamble playing Friday in the first place, but for my money a half-dead Friday would be better than some of the Reading players who stayed on.

Reading Evening Post, 5 April 1974

. . . Star striker Robin Friday, pulled off on Wednesday after he got out of his sick-bed to play, is still suffering the effects of a bad bout of flu . . .

DAVID DOWNS: I would say that he worked as hard at the end of the game as he did at the start. No disrespect to players in the Sunday leagues, but because they are so keen on their football and they are doing it for the love of it, they put 100 per cent in. That was Robin's attitude. He was out there to enjoy the game and put everything he had into every minute of every game he played. If a club had tried to calm him down and make him more orthodox or make him conform more to the acceptable patterns of play and behaviour, then I think you would have taken all that flair and improvisation away from him.

Reading Evening Post, 6 April 1974
Reading 0 Scunthorpe 0
. . . Robin Friday passed himself fit to play just before the game, and was soon in the wars, taking a blow in the stomach from Simpkin in the first minute. Shortly afterwards, Friday was fouled again as he tried to break through from the right . . . Around the half-hour mark Reading began to play with a little more cohesion and a great move involving Cummings, Butler, Youlden, Chapell, Habbin and Stuckey ended with Friday heading over the cross-bar. A quickly taken corner on the left created another chance when Stuckey fired a fierce shot across goal and Friday sought to power another diving header inches over the top . . . Then Friday fired in a fierce low shot which Barnard saved at the far post, and Acker was lucky not to concede a penalty when he deliberately handled a Friday header . . .

Reading Evening Post, 12 April 1974
Reading 4 Torquay United 0
. . . In a game which never reached the heights, we saw the familiar spectacle of Robin Friday being kicked all over the place and finally off the pitch . . . Torquay's Dave Kennedy joined the long list of

players booked for fouling Friday . . . Seven minutes after half-time Kennedy was cautioned for bringing down the ex-Hayes man for the third time and Friday immediately limped out of the game . . . This was a great shame, for the long-haired striker was beginning to recapture the red-hot form he showed when he first joined the club . . . Goal number two in the 34th minute was probably the best of the lot . . . Friday went past four men in a brilliant run, and when his left-foot shot on the run appeared to be covered on the line, Chapell came racing in to slide it into the opposite corner. Two minutes later, Friday lost the chance of a goal for himself when a mix-up over a short goal-kick left the Torquay goal empty. But, under pressure and at a narrowing angle, Friday couldn't quite get the ball to run for him . . .

CHARLIE HURLEY: He was tremendously outspoken and we used to have a lot of arguments after the games. If there was one thing he hated, it was him giving 100 per cent and his team-mates shirking. That really made him furious. He loved the ball, so you could always find Robin. There are different ways of not wanting the ball, ways of saying 'no thank you'. It is a well-known fact in the game that Robin was never like that.

Reading Evening Post, 12 April 1974
Rotherham 1 Reading 1

Reading Evening Post, 15 April 1974
Reading 1 Torquay 1
. . . As in Saturday's match at Rotherham, Reading fell behind to an early goal and equalised pretty well straightaway with a Bruce Stuckey penalty to end with the honours even . . . Within a couple of minutes of the penalty, Robin Friday went just wide with a header and Reading continued to create the better scoring chances with Friday and Percy Freeman going close to grabbing the winner on several occasions. However, Robin Friday managed to get booked,

his second caution since joining the club . . . This time it was for taking a kick at Mahoney, the Torquay keeper . . .

Reading Evening Post, 20 April 1974

Reading 1 Stockport 1

. . . One of the club's very best fans tells me it was the worst game he had seen on the ground for 40 years. The level of entertainment was so low as to be a public disgrace. The game had about as much excitement as a marathon race between two unfit snails. A shot by Percy Freeman was so inaccurate that it finished in the back garden of a house in Suffolk Road, and for all I know the ball is still there.

Reading Evening Post, 22 April 1974

Reading 3 Chester 0

. . . Two amazing goals by Percy Freeman in the space of an incredible 74 seconds gave Reading's faithful long-suffering fans an exciting finale to the season at Elm Park last night. Although the smallest gate for a league game at the ground for two years, that faith was demonstrated at the end by youngsters who ran on to the pitch at the end calling for Charlie Hurley. Those fans who saw promotion thrown away at home matches last night witnessed the second half played with the sort of aggressive attacking that has been so conspicuously lacking most of the season.

Reading Evening Post, 23 April 1974

. . . Footballer George Best left court a free man and without a stain on his character today. Prosecution offered no evidence against him at London's Marylebone Court on two charges of stealing property of Miss Marjorie Wallace, the deposed Miss World . . . This was bearded Best's third appearance at the court.

Reading Evening Post, 26 April 1974

. . . Three Reading players will be under orders to be on their best behaviour when the Elm Park visit Chester for the final Fourth

Division game of the season on Saturday. Robin Friday, Stewart Henderson and Dick Habbin could all miss the first two games of next season if they are booked at Seal End Road . . . Friday is the man nearest the danger mark. His caution at Torquay on Easter Monday was his third of the season. He had one outstanding from Hayes and now has ten penalty points against him. Said manager Charlie Hurley, 'I don't want anybody messing up my plans for the start of next season.'

. . . Attendances at Elm Park were up this season but by nowhere near enough for Reading Football Club to break even . . .

Reading Evening Post, 27 April 1974
Chester 0 Reading 0.
. . . Aggravating Reading picked a pretty stupid time to play some of their best football of the season. In the second half of last Wednesday's game against Chester at Elm Park and the first half of Saturday's return at Seal End Road they were playing some of their best attacking football this season . . . but they couldn't score . . . The worst culprit was Robin Friday . . . In the build-up he was at his brilliant best, time and time again drifting by a string of defenders . . . But when it came to what seemed the easy bit, his final passes and shots let him down completely . . .

Friday failed to maintain the early burst of scoring he enjoyed shortly after coming to Reading and in this game he really ought to have brought his long, barren run to an end. His last effort, which hit the side-netting near the angle of the post and crossbar, was so close that some people in the stand thought that it was a goal that had been disallowed . . . However, the game petered down to yet another draw, Reading's 19th of the season . . .

Reading Evening Post, 1 May 1974
. . . Sir Alf Ramsey was sacked today after an 11-year reign as England soccer manager . . .

4 May 1974
FA Cup final: Liverpool 3 Newcastle 0

Reading Evening Post, 16 May 1974
. . . Reading's tough-guy striker, Robin Friday, played the last four
league matches this season with a chipped ankle bone and he didn't
know a thing about it. Elm Park boss Charlie Hurley revealed today
that the result of x-rays on the ankle after he injured it in the Good
Friday game with Torquay at home showed a chipped bone. Hurley
told me, 'We allowed him to go to his own doctor and have some
x-rays. He never complained but just went out there and got on
with the job. He's a real tough nut.'

SHEILA FRIDAY: He played with a cracked bone in his foot, didn't
he?

ALF FRIDAY: One night a geezer gave him a whack and he went up
to the hospital and they said he had been playing with a break in
his ankle – well, they said it could have been any sort of time. He
ended up on crutches. He was funny with them. He used to
come down the stairs like a monkey. He was a livewire.

Reading Evening Post, 16 May 1974
. . . Stan Bowles has walked out of the England squad. He is thought
to be upset after being substituted by Joe Mercer in Wednesday's
international.

Reading Evening Post, 17 May 1974
. . . Police reports of a punch-up after a Reading journalist and his
colleague tracked down missing England soccer star Stan Bowles at
White City Greyhound Stadium last night . . . A reporter traced
Bowles to the stadium bar where he refused to comment on his
absence from the England squad. George Best was given a leggy
welcome by a group of musical show chorus girls when he arrived

in Johannesburg today to play for a South African First Division club . . .

Reading Evening Post, 21 May 1974

. . . Man Friday on the move. But don't worry, fans, it's only to be near Elm Park. Manager Charlie Hurley wants the 21-year-old to move to Reading so he'll be nearer the club. But Robin, who was an instant hit with the fans when he joined the club in January, is not too keen to leave his 17th-floor flat in Park Road North, Acton. The club has already offered him a furnished flat but he wants somewhere with room to exercise his 18-month-old alsatian, Ziggy. Robin said last night, 'The boss suggested that I swap the council flat in Acton for a council house in Reading, but I don't think many people would be keen to swap a flat for a house. Anyway, I'm quite content to stay here rather than move. I don't like Reading as a town much either. If I was gonna move it would have to be a house with a garden, cos she's a big dog and needs a lot of room. But I'm not very keen because I've got all my own furniture and a new place would mean new carpets and things and a mortgage, and at the moment it only takes half an hour to travel to Reading three or four times a week.'

He's not sure what price he would want to pay for a house which would have to accommodate him, his wife Maxine and their five-year-old daughter Nicola, not forgetting the dog. It would depend on what mortgage he would get on his earnings of around £45 a week. He would have less difficulty if he followed his summer trade as a roofing asphalter where he can earn £100 a week. 'But money is not everything,' says Robin. 'I like playing football and I would just have to see what was going.'

. . . There is a game fixed up before the new Football League season starts (on 17 August) at Hayes on Wednesday, 7 August. Manager Charlie Hurley agreed to take his side to the Isthmian League club as a thank-you gesture for the signing of Robin Friday.

Reading Evening Post, 3 June 1974

Almost a third of young people questioned in a Reading public opinion survey have taken the drug marijuana. Some 40 per cent said they had tried LSD . . .

. . . Supergroups Focus and Traffic are among the groups topping the bill at the this year's Reading Rock Festival over the August Bank Holiday. Also among the bill-toppers are the Sensational Alex Harvey Band . . .

Reading Evening Post, 12 July 1974

. . . The 1974–75 soccer season opened at Elm Park today with a few old familiar faces present but a handful of players missing. Absent on the first day back were Bruce Stuckey and Andy Alleyne (both still on holiday), Bob Lenarduzzi (who's in Canada) and Robin Friday (who's having tattoos removed from his fingers).

MAURICE EVANS, READING COACH: It was amazing when Charlie Hurley brought me back to Reading in 1974. He said, 'We've got a player named Robin Friday here. He is unbelievable. You'll love him.' I didn't know Robin. I'd been up in Shrewsbury, so I said, 'I'll look forward to that.' Pre-season training started in early July – no Robin Friday. So I said to Charlie, 'What's happened with Robin?' He said, 'I don't know, I haven't got a clue.' Eventually, Charlie came in and said, 'I've found him! He's been in a hippie commune in Cornwall for the summer.' He'd just decided to come back. As it happened we were playing Watford in a private game at Adwets, which was our training ground. Now Robin had done absolutely no training at all – you can imagine what sort of state he was in – and he was the best player on the field by a mile. I couldn't believe it. He was unbelievable.

Reading Evening Post, 12 July 1974

. . . Bill Shankly shocked the soccer world today with the bombshell news that he is handing over the reins at Anfield and retiring . . .

Reading Evening Post, 17 July 1974

. . . Reading Football Club lost over £16,000 last year and they are now over £79,000 in debt.

Reading Evening Post, 24 July 1974

. . . Now Hurley is awaiting the return to training of Robin Friday who made such a big impact when he joined the club in the second half of last season. Following an operation for the removal of tattoos, Friday still has his right hand in plaster and is now expected back at the club next Monday. That will leave him only one week to get fully fit before the first pre-season friendly against Portsmouth at Elm Park . . .

. . . George Best shook hands with Dunstable Town chairman Keith Cheesman in the early hours of this morning and said, 'I'm ready to join Dunstable.' Best added, 'All I ever wanted to do was play football and that's what I can do at Dunstable. There will be no pressures on me and I will be able to play football for the love of the game.' And, added Barry Fry, 'How can you put in words what it means getting George Best for Dunstable? It will be a bigger boost for the club than having Frank Sinatra sing at half-time . . .'

★ ★ ★

MAURICE EVANS, READING COACH: Charlie said, 'We've got to get him down to Reading where we can see him, we know what's happening and we've got a fair idea of what's going on.' I said, 'Charlie, I don't know if that's such a good idea because all the idiots in Reading will grab onto him and he'll end up with them.'

ROD LEWINGTON: Reading was a town full of characters in those days and Robin was the kingpin of all these characters.

CHARLIE HURLEY: We got him a flat around the corner from the club and I have to say it wasn't the cleanest flat I ever visited. There were things we had to do to get him straightened out – like taking money out of his wages to pay the bills. Even then it didn't matter that much, because all the guys who would come round to collect money owed were real big Robin Friday fans.

SYD SIMMONDS, FRIEND: I made friends with Robin when he came to play for Reading. I used to go down there because I knew some of the players and I had a player's pass. Robin moved down from London into 193 Tilehurst Road, two doors down from the Royal Rendezvous club. That was a club flat and I moved in with him.

ROD LEWINGTON: He did get involved with a lot of guys who probably took advantage of him – not by poncing money off him but by basking in his reflected glory. They'd take him out on these marathon drinking sessions and he didn't have the willpower to say no.

★ ★ ★

Reading Evening Post, 6 August 1974
Reading 1 Portsmouth 0
. . . Friday missed a couple of good chances when clear on his own and he must be the most frustrating man to play with. But take him away from the team and the entire entertainment value would virtually disappear.

Reading Evening Post, 7 August 1974
Reading 1 Hayes 1

Reading Evening Post, 8 August 1974
. . .The turbulent presidency of Richard Nixon ended today, finally

destroyed by the Watergate scandal.

. . . A show of force in Reading today as fears rise of violence out on the terraces at Elm Park. They are not saying just how many officers are being drafted in for the pre-season friendly against Oxford United, but according to a spokesman the fans will be closely watched from the time they arrive in the town to the time they leave.

Reading Evening Post, 10 August 1974

. . . Reading's ace striker, Robin Friday, missed today's friendly local game against Oxford United at Elm Park. Friday, who has shown up so well in Reading's other two pre-season friendlies, against Portsmouth and Hayes, is ruled out by a painful boil on his knee. It was a big blow to manager Charlie Hurley and the fans.

Reading Evening Post, 16 August 1974

. . . John Murray makes his début for Reading in their big opening Fourth Division match at Cambridge United at Elm Park tomorrow and the signing of this Bury midfield player could not come at a better time since manager Charlie Hurley's injury-ravaged squad is down to its minimum of 12.

JOHN MURRAY, PLAYER: I came from Burnley because I beat up the manager there. I don't know – Charlie Hurley must have had a thing for bad boys that season.

MAURICE EVANS: Robin never had any money. I was always lending him money but he always paid me back. He was always looking for money for something, like a taxi fare.

ROD LEWINGTON: If you said to Robin, as a lot of people round town did, 'Give us a fiver, mate,' he would give it to you and then forget all about it. He wouldn't say two weeks later, 'Where's that fiver?' As far as he was concerned the money was gone. A fiver is worth what 20 quid is now, but he would just forget about it.

JOHN MURRAY: His friends were the taxi-drivers, the nutcases. They'd take him into clubs, put him in a cupboard with a lass and let him get on with it.

ROD LEWINGTON: Churchills was probably the worst club that has ever been in Reading. It was a dreadful place over at Simpson's Junction. It was a room above a bank with just a bar and the bare essentials – a dancefloor and tapes for the disco. It was a dreadful place but you could drink there all night long, which was the only attraction. All the guys who went there were banned from everywhere else. Anyway, I met Robin in the pub one night and after the pub shut we went to Churchills. Robin was wearing this long overcoat and hobnail boots. So we stroll in, he goes over to the dance floor and takes off his overcoat and he is stark bollock naked under it. All he had on was this pair of hobnail boots. Incredible. There were times as well when he would take a woman into one of the rooms and we would stand outside to make sure nobody else could get in. It was the only club in Reading that would stand for that kind of behaviour.

★ ★ ★

Reading Evening Post, 17 August 1974
Reading 2 Cambridge United 0
. . . Reading new boy John Murray had a dream début when he scored a penalty and set up the second goal against Cambridge at Elm Park . . . After 30 minutes Reading went ahead from the penalty spot following the most bizarre incident. Cambridge goalkeeper Smith went down to take a long back-pass and unaccountably allowed an easy ball to slip from his grasp. Friday raced in to try and

place the loose ball into the empty goal only for Smith to grab the Reading man's legs and pull him down . . .

Most of the fireworks came as usual from Robin Friday, who entertained the crowd and frustrated the Cambridge players with his highly individual brand of skills. His promise was one of the high spots of the game which wilted a little under a hot sun in the second half. Reading must think that although this was not really their best there could be no question of who deserved to win.

JOHN MURRAY: The first thing he did when he moved into his flat was to paint the walls black. He said there was nothing worse than getting stoned and looking at strange wallpaper patterns.

Reading Evening Post, 21 August 1974
Reading 0 Brighton 0
. . . Manager Charlie Hurley said, 'We were brilliant, great. But the cruel truth is that all the excellence in the football is of no use if you can't get the ball into the net.'

Reading Evening Post, 24 August 1974
Rotherham United 2 Reading 1
. . . Reading equalised Philip's first-half goal with a fine header by Robin Friday, but little was seen of the Reading attack, in which Habbin and Friday were fighting a hopeless battle against the odds.

Reading Evening Post, 24 August 1974
Violence erupted today at Windsor Great Park when the police tried to break up the Free Pop Park Festival. Savage fighting broke out when armoured police stormed the stage where a large number of fans had gathered . . .

SYD SIMMONDS: He was into heavy metal. The Alex Harvey Band

– mad for that. Led Zeppelin. His records were his pride and joy. You weren't allowed to touch any of them. As soon as you got in the flat, even if it was three in the morning, the first thing would be to get the music playing. We had an old boy living below us, Bill Smith, the ex-groundsman at Reading. He was coming up to 80 and he had a dog's life in that flat. Pounding music, people knocking on the door, girls throwing stones at the windows. Poor old sod.

Reading Evening Post, 29 August 1974
Brighton 2 Reading 2
. . . They have to meet for a third time to decide their League Cup first round game next Tuesday. Firstly, so long as there can be football such as this the game still has, contrary to popular current opinion, a great future. Also, if Reading can maintain this level of performance to the end of season they will walk promotion . . .

. . . You see them here, you see them there, you see them almost everywhere. What are they? Why, frisbees of course. At the Reading Festival, frisbees were seen for one of the first times.

Reading Evening Post, 2 September 1974
Reading 3 Northampton 2
. . . If Reading had not replied within three minutes with a goal superbly conceived by Robin Friday and scored by Dick Habbin, they may never have got back into it . . .

Reading Evening Post, 4 September 1974
Reading 0 Brighton 0
. . . It's 0–0 again. So where's it all going to end? Best chances went Reading's way in the second half. Friday wastefully slammed over just after the break and was then awarded an indirect free-kick when two defenders blocked his way with one of the trio obviously handling . . . Friday went close three times but the best chance of the

lot went to Brighton substitute Marlow. Friday spoilt a fine evening's work by getting himself booked for a late tackle for the second time in four days.

Reading Evening Post, 6 September 1974
Brighton 2 Reading 3
. . . When Murray's shot hit the post, this time jubilant Robin Friday was there, sliding on his back to push it into the goal. When it was all over Friday lay stretched out on the turf . . .

CHARLIE HURLEY: We played a 4-3-3 formation and it was a great team at Elm Park. Opponents could never get through us. We used to give Robin a fairly free rein because he was a grafter. We had a lad called Dick Habbin who was a great runner off the ball, and Robin used to drop deep and find Dick with some great balls. We had Gordon Cummings on the right wing and we had a great defence.

Reading Evening Post, 7 September 1974
Scunthorpe 0 Reading 1
. . . It was Robin Friday's match at Scunthorpe this afternoon. He headed the goal that gave Reading a win and turned in a star display. The only goal of the game came in the 19th minute. Dave Moreline floated in a free-kick from the left wing and Friday got to it first to back head it over the advancing keeper into the empty net. It was Friday's fourth goal of the season and his third in consecutive games. Friday could have had a second goal in injury-time when he rattled the cross-bar.

Reading Evening Post, 9 September 1974
. . . Charlie Hurley today denied that First Division Sheffield United have made an approach for his star striker Robin Friday. United watched Friday for the sixth time on Saturday when he scored the only goal of the game at Scunthorpe. He first impressed them at

Barnsley last season in only his second Football League game when he was still an amateur. United assistant manager John Shaw also watched Friday head a fine goal at Rotherham a fortnight ago, but the Reading manager said, 'Apart from two enquiries about Youlden I have not had any bid for players at all this season. However, it doesn't surprise me if people are watching Friday. He's a damn good player.' As Friday is not officially available for transfer, the club cannot name the fee they would want for him. If Sheffield were to move in with an offer I don't imagine Reading would let him go for much less than £100,000.

CHARLIE HURLEY: I was headhunted by Sheffield United when they were in the First Division but I had always promised Reading I wouldn't do anything until I got them promotion. I've always had principles. They're quite expensive to have at the moment.

* * *

MAURICE EVANS: We used to go by train from Euston up north for various games. Robin would meet us at Euston Station. One time, he turned up in a pair of jeans, high-heel crocodile boots, a black T-shirt with 'Deep Purple' written all across it in mauve. And nothing else, nothing at all. We would walk into these hotels and people are going, 'Who is this fellow coming in?'

CHARLIE HURLEY: He tried very hard to do what I wanted him to do and I was clever enough to realise that he was trying very hard. But he had this wild streak. He loved a drink, he was a good-looking lad so I presume he didn't have too much trouble with women, and I think he went around with quite a wild bunch. If you give yourself marks out of ten for getting a guy to do something for you within that environment, I would have given myself five or six out of ten.

MAURICE EVANS: He loved people. He was great company, Robin, and seeing as he was one of the top sportsmen in Reading at the time, everyone wanted to know him. We tried to protect him, talking and talking to him, just saying, 'Robin, realise what you've got – great ability – just settle down, get yourself fit and you can go anywhere.' But then he'd laugh and say, 'You must be bloody joking. I don't want to be training every day and running round and round the pitch. Give me the ball and I'll do anything. But I don't want to work.'

Reading Evening Post, 12 September 1974
Reading 4 Rotherham 2
. . . Arsenal manager Bertie Mee was at Elm Park last night and was 'probably watching Robin Friday or Dick Habbin', said a Highbury spokesman today.

An hour of probably the best football that Reading have played for five years swept Rotherham out of the League Cup in Elm Park last night. The first in the 11th minute followed a superb piece of work by Robin Friday. Running diagonally through the defence, he split Rotherham wide open with a sudden backheel straight into the path of Stewart Henderson. The Reading skipper unleashed a fierce left-foot drive which Rotherham keeper Jim McDonaugh could not hold, and Dick Habbin was on it like lightning to net. Robin Friday was there for number two. Showing utter contempt for McDonaugh, he side-footed the ball within inches of the keeper for his fourth goal in consecutive games. Victory assured, Reading slacked off.

Mr Mee left nearly half an hour from the end when Reading were winning 4–0. Charlie Hurley said today that Arsenal did not make any enquiries for any of his players.

Reading Evening Post, 12 September 1974
. . . Stan Bowles, QPR's controversial transfer-listed forward, is

included in new England manager Don Revie's squad for a get-together in Manchester in ten days' time. Only last May Bowles walked out on an England international. His excuse was that he did not like flying.

Reading Evening Post, 14 September 1974
Reading 3 Newport 0
. . . Super Reading romped home at Elm Park this afternoon, crushing their visitors Newport County. Goals from Habbin, Taylor (a penalty) and Friday accounted for them. Reading made it 3–0. Taylor sent over a corner from the left which found Youlden flying high above the defence to head down into the six-yard box where Friday flung himself full length among the flying boots to nod in his sixth goal of the season.

. . . Six-goal Reading strikers Robin Friday and Dick Habbin stand proudly at the head of the Football League's leading goalscorers list. In a remarkable achievement for Reading, Friday and Habbin have both scored more than anyone else in Division Four. No wonder a fan telephoned the *Evening Post* last week threatening to burn down Elm Park if the club ever sold Friday . . .

Reading Evening Post, 18 September 1974
. . . George Foreman has pulled out of the heavyweight title fight in Zaire. Foreman cut his right eye during training . . .

Reading Evening Post, 18 September 1974
Reading 1 Crewe 1
So it's happened again for the umpteenth time. A big crowd, a big occasion and there's nothing more certain than that Reading will flop . . . it is as predictable as night following day . . .

Reading's first-minute goal was scored by Alan Taylor but it was also reported that Stewart Henderson and star striker Robin Friday are very doubtful for Reading's visit to Exeter on Saturday. A big worry is Friday who is visiting his doctor in London today for an x-ray on the ankle he hurt in last night's draw with Crewe. Friday limped off for a couple of minutes near the end of the game after banging his foot into the ground. There were fears at Elm Park that he may have cracked a bone.

SYD SIMMONDS: He never wore shinpads. He'd come out with his socks up and within five minutes of the game starting they'd be round his ankles. Shirt hanging out, which they never used to like, long hair, and tattoos of the words 'mild' and 'bitter' on his chest.

Reading Evening Post, 20 September 1974
. . . Reading skipper Stewart Henderson misses tomorrow's match at Exeter but today there was still a chance that the club's other casualty, star striker Robin Friday, will be fit. The x-ray Friday had on his ankle revealed that there was nothing broken, but a final decision on his fitness will be taken tomorrow morning. If Friday is found unfit his place would go to one of three – Les Chapell, Gordon Cumming or Bruce Stuckey.

. . . Reading received a tremendous boost before the start of their match at Exeter when Robin Friday was declared fit. Friday, the extrovert of Elm Park and a much sought-after player this season, successfully came through a stiff fitness test this morning. 'I am delighted to say that Robin is fit,' said manager Charlie Hurley before the Reading party set off by rail for the West Country.

. . . Three soccer fans from the Reading area were arrested by police at Exeter this afternoon . . . A crowd of more than 20 fans gathered and in the subsequent struggle with the civil police one youth was found with a lavatory fitting.

Reading Evening Post, 23 September 1974
Exeter 0 Reading 2

Reading Evening Post, 26 September 1974
Chester 2 Reading 0

... Reading's nine-game unbeaten run came to a sorry end at a wet, cold and windy Seal End Road last night. The second-minute goal knocked the stuffing out of Reading and they never really suggested they would recover a point despite a strong second-half rally. Reading had a golden chance to rescue something when Robin Friday was put through by Bob Lenarduzzi a minute before the end of full time. But Friday tried to be too clever and the opportunity disappeared. Only Robin Friday, working extremely hard as always, and Lenarduzzi gave reasonably good accounts of themselves. But it was difficult to see who could have impressed Liverpool manager Bob Paisley watching for himself after sending a scout to Elm Park early on in the season. And Preston manager Bobby Charlton spying on his League Cup opponents saw just how hard it is to get a result at Chester. Nobody has won there for over a year and Reading never looked like spoiling that record.

Saturday night TV, 28 September 1974
BBC 1: *Kojak, Match of the Day* and *Parkinson*
ITV: *Hawaii Five-O, Upstairs Downstairs, Up the Junction*

Reading Evening Post, 30 September 1974
Reading 4 Southport 1

... Reading goal king Robin Friday stands accused of selfishness towards his club and its fans. Friday, who was booked for the third time this season at Elm Park on Saturday, is letting down more than just himself. He is also selling short his club who may now have to do without his services for two matches as well as the fans who enjoy seeing him play for Reading. By his own admission he was lucky not to be sent off against Southport and he almost left his team-mates the extra burden of playing with ten men. The ridiculous thing about it is that Friday was in trouble for three completely unnecessary fouls. He has no need whatsoever to charge into goalkeepers or trip opponents. The reason he doesn't need to do this is that he has far too much ability for that. He can win through by pure skill alone, as he proved once again with a well-taken hat-trick, his first in the league. Friday desperately wants to win promotion with Reading but he won't help that cause by getting himself suspended. He had eight penalty points before Saturday's match and has almost certainly increased that to 12, which makes his suspension automatic with his stupid lunge at Southport keeper Edmunds. That means a two-match ban — and the games he will miss (unless he decides to appeal) could hardly be more important: the League Cup-tie against Burnley and a home league match against Fourth Division leaders Shrewsbury. Friday's goals, in the 28th, 36th and 74th minutes, showed just what a vital member of the team he is. His first two were almost carbon copies of each other: chasing through long headers, first by Tommy Youlden and then by Barry Wagstaff, and pushing the ball out of the reach of the advancing keeper. Southport manager Alan Ball thought both goals were offside but the referee and linesman didn't. Dick Habbin's cross at the end of a fine move was so inch-perfect that Friday only had to touch the ball into the empty net with his head for his third.

Friday has now scored nine goals this season and jointly tops the league list with Aston Villa's Ray Graydon. He collected £5 from chairman Duncan Vincent for a bet about the hat-trick and £3 from Charlie Hurley. He faces a showdown with his manager about his disciplinary problems later in the week.

Southport's reaction to Friday's antics were little short of disgusting. When he elbowed the goalkeeper, Edmunds pretended to be near death's door until the Reading man was booked. And when he playfully punched Johnson on the chin the bearded midfield player, who had been guilty of a string of fouls, did his best to get Friday sent off. Southport themselves had a player dismissed, 19-year-old right-back Alan Kershaw getting an early bath for tripping Habbin.

CHARLIE HURLEY: We didn't need anyone else up front – they couldn't get the ball off him. He was one of those guys who could beat five players easily. And the worst thing you can do in football is take the piss.

Reading Evening Post, 1 October 1974
Rochdale 0 Reading 2
... An enormous squad of leading managers and scouts saw Reading's triumphant progress to the top of the Fourth Division last night. The extremely interested onlookers included Aston Villa manager Ron Saunders, one of Friday's biggest fans, Don Howe of West Brom, Tony Book of Manchester City, Gordon Milne of Coventry and Leeds' chief scout Tony Collins. The VIP lounge looked more packed than the terraces, although the game attracted Rochdale's biggest crowd for several months. Both Friday and Habbin did an enormous amount of donkey work at the front of what was virtually a 4-4-2 set-up. In fact, Habbin must have done his chances of a move to a big club a power of good with a brilliant performance, as well as scoring his eighth goal of the season. But individuals shouldn't be allowed to take prevalence over what was again a fine team effort ...

We have *Match of the Day,* Goal of the Month and Goal of the Season but this effort followed what must be a strong candidate for Pass of the Season title. The man who made it was none other than Reading goalkeeper Death. Dashing out to the edge of his area to boot the ball away from Carrick he hammered a massive kick upfield. It may have been intended to clear the stand but the ball stayed in play and came down at the feet of the unmarked Friday deep inside the Rochdale half. With three men up against three, Friday raced down the wing, and although he missed his low cross, Habbin was on hand to stroke the ball in.

Division Four, 1 October 1974

1. Reading
2. Shrewsbury
3. Rotherham

For two of the Reading players, Robin Friday and Barry Wagstaff, the forthcoming friendly against Arsenal will be their third match in three days as there are only ten fit players available for the reserves at Fulham yesterday. Manager Charlie Hurley asked for volunteers and both Friday and Wagstaff immediately offered to play. Both men played for 45 minutes each and were rewarded by helping the reserves to their first win of the season. The pair had returned from the 2–0 win at Rochdale in the early hours of yesterday morning and today Hurley said, 'This is the kind of spirit that will take the club places. Arsenal's side includes four full internationals, Alan Ball, Brian Kidd, John Radford and Peter Storey.

All eyes will again be on Friday and Dick Habbin with nine and eight goals respectively, the most successful striking duo in the entire Football League.

MAURICE EVANS: When I was in charge of the reserves we were playing Crystal Palace and Robin came down. Of course he had no money so Charlie said, 'Give him a lift back to London on the coach.' I said, 'Yeah, all right.' Then Robin asked to play. Charlie said, 'I don't really want you to play, Robin, you might get injured.' He said, 'I won't bloody well get injured, let me play.' I was saying, 'Charlie, let him play.' You can imagine why. So anyway out he goes. He hadn't even cleaned his boots – they were absolutely caked in mud. The game started and Robin did two or three unbelievable things. Terry Venables was there at Palace and he lent over to us in the dugout and said, 'Who the bloody hell is that?' Robin was brilliant that day. Just playing in a game like that because he loved football. He really did. He loved it.

ALF FRIDAY: They reckon loads of people were watching him but you don't know. Terry Venables wanted him when he was at Palace. Venables wanted a player exchange, though, because they couldn't put up the money.

Reading Evening Post, 3 October 1974
Reading 0 Arsenal 2
. . . Reading star striker Robin Friday and manager Charlie Hurley meet tomorrow to decide whether to appeal against the booking which threatens to rule Friday out of next week's vital matches against Burnley and Shrewsbury. It was confirmed today that Friday received four points for his caution against Southport last night so he now has collected 12 this season. If he decides not to appeal, he will automatically be banned from the club's two home matches next week. Hurley received the report from referee Les Burden today and said afterwards, 'I am not at all happy with his view of the incident. I will discuss this with Robin tomorrow and then we will come to a decision whether to appeal.' Friday, who was booked for a foul on Southport goalkeeper Derek Edmunds, was also cautioned against Northampton and in the third match with Brighton. I have a feeling Friday, whose nine goals make him the second-highest scorer in the league, will go ahead with an appeal to the FA disciplinary committee. If Friday doesn't appeal, Saturday night's match with Torquay will be his last for 11 days.

Reading Evening Post, 4 October 1974
. . . Manager Charlie Hurley confirmed today that he will definitely appeal against the booking which Friday received against Southport last Friday. The Reading chief was not satisfied with the referee Les Burden's report of the incident.

Reading Evening Post, 7 October 1974
Torquay 2 Reading 1

Reading Evening Post, 10 October 1974
Reading 1 Burnley 2
. . . Unlucky Reading went out of the League Cup, beaten 2–1 by
First Division Burnley in the third round. A bumper crowd of 14,250
saw Reading outplay their opponents for most of the game before
losing to two late goals.

Reading Evening Post, 14 October 1974
Reading 1 Shrewsbury 2
. . . Reading players are to pick up £60 bonuses after their shocking
display at Elm Park on Saturday. The reason? Their position in the
top four after 12 matches as part of the club incentive scheme to get
out of Division Four.

CHARLIE HURLEY: You get all different types of people in football
who are looking for an excuse to have a go. The cliché is, 'Well,
if he does it so I can do it.' Which they don't because it's not
their nature. If someone complained about Robin, I'd say, 'Okay
then, let me ask you a question. When Robin scores the goals on
Saturdays and you get a win bonus, do you want me to take that
away? I can do that easily. I can put Robin on the transfer list.
Now you go home tonight and think very hard about it and
when you come back in the morning tell me if you want me to
get rid of Robin or not.' They'd come back in the morning and
– apart from one player – would say, 'Yes, we want Robin to
stay.' Sometimes I'd tell Robin, 'You're a real bastard off the
pitch. Now imagine what you'd be like if you were a nice lad?'
He'd say, 'But I might not be the same player.' And maybe he
was right.

SYD SIMMONDS: His team-mates didn't really worry about it
because he'd done the business on a Wednesday night or a
Saturday afternoon. Tommy Youlden was a bit offish because he

was a dead straight man who never smoked, never drank and never went out.

DAVID DOWNS, READING FC HISTORIAN: A pal of mine who played with him at the time was Tommy Youlden and he wouldn't have anything to do with Robin. Players like him didn't like Robin's lifestyle – not because they were snobs but because his lifestyle was so strange. I had a lot of time for Robin. I was a great fan of what he did on the football field and I thought his personality was very genuine. He would do anything for you if he could. He would give out free tickets before games and I'm sure he felt a lot happier talking to fans than to directors or some of the players.

CHARLIE HURLEY: You should have seen him with the directors. Hilarious. 'How you doing, Frank?' This is to Frank Waller, chairman of the club. Sir Ernie Harrison: 'All right Ernie!' Frank Waller said to me, 'He shouldn't be calling me Frank.' I said, 'Why, what's your name then?' When you think about it, why should you call someone Mister? None of us are called Mister. Unless you are named Mister and I have never heard of anyone called that.

Reading Evening Post, 16 October 1974
. . . Nine-goal Robin Friday has to attend a hearing in London. Friday is appearing in an FA disciplinary committee meeting at the FA headquarters at Lancaster Gate on Monday, 28 October. He will be appealing against his booking against Southport last month which brought the total of penalty points against him to twelve.

Reading Evening Post, 19 October 1974
Mansfield 1 Reading 1
. . . Goal ace Dick Habbin was Reading's hero again at Mansfield today. The Fourth Division's top scorer smashed his 11th goal this

season to earn Reading a surprise point. Just before the interval Reading burst into life again when Friday did extremely well to get in behind the defence on the left. His acute angled shot was deflected across the penalty area and when Reading quit the attack to gain on the other flank Murray went close. Right on half-time Friday hooked a volley well over the bar from the edge of the box.

Reading Evening Post, 25 October 1974
. . . Three Reading players were sent home today with colds and all must be considered slightly doubtful for tomorrow's home Fourth Division match with Barnsley. Skipper Stewart Henderson, Dave Moreline and Robin Friday are the three involved.

Reading Evening Post, 26 October 1974
Reading 0 Barnsley 3
. . . Two goals in the first five minutes sent Reading crashing to a disastrous defeat at the hands of lowly Barnsley at Elm Park this afternoon. In their fifth game without a win, Reading slipped further away from the Fourth Division promotion race. The most important date for Reading next week is off the pitch and not on it. That's on Monday when Robin Friday appears before the FA disciplinary committee. Friday is appealing against the last of his three bookings this season for a foul on Southport's goalkeeper. If his appeal is unsuccessful, Friday will have to sit out a two-match ban. That ban would most likely start a week later so Friday would miss the club's big excursion to away games at Hartlepool and Workington. Friday will be represented by manager Charlie Hurley who has revealed, 'I have got something up my sleeve for the hearing.'

CHARLIE HURLEY: We used to come back from travelling away, stop for fish and chips, a couple of pints if we had won, a pint if we lost and for a very good win you might get three pints. It was a nice atmosphere, it was always good to get away from the razzmatazz and have a few pints. Occasionally we would have a few drinks on the coach and Robin would always drink faster than anyone else. I think it was because it was free.

Reading Evening Post, 28 October 1974

. . . Reading striker Robin Friday was hoping today that much troubled goalkeeper Derek Edmunds would save him from suspension. Edmunds was the man Friday was booked for fouling when he played for Southport at Elm Park last month. This afternoon Friday was appealing against that caution in an FA disciplinary committee in London and Edmunds was expected to give his evidence for him. Friday was banking on Edmunds to save him from a two-match ban. If his appeal fails he will immediately be suspended. Ironically, Friday did not help Edmunds' career when he banged the hat-trick past him in Reading's 4–1 win.

Reading Evening Post, 29 October 1974

. . . Reading striker Robin Friday missed his FA disciplinary committee appeal yesterday because he was in bed suffering from flu and bronchitis. But the illness may turn out to be a blessing in disguise since goalkeeper Derek Edmunds, Friday's star witness, may not have got to London for the case yesterday and he could be available when it is finally heard. Manager Charlie Hurley said: 'When Robin phoned to say he was ill, he was obviously not himself. He was in bed with a cold on the day before the match. It may be a help that the hearing was put off because we don't know if Edmunds would have made it yesterday. He was struggling to get off work. Now we don't know when it will be held. It could be a few weeks before they can all get their witnesses together again.'

Reading Evening Post, 30 October 1974

. . . Muhammad Ali, the man who believes in miracles, produced one today to dethrone George Foreman as world heavyweight boxing champion with an eighth-round knock-out. The fearsome Foreman, unbeaten in his previous 40 fights and regarded as one of the hardest hitters in heavyweight history, was reduced to a shambling wreck by Ali's dazzling artistry and relentless psychological warfare.

Reading Evening Post, 31 October 1974
. . . Robin Friday is back in training, but John Murray is unlikely to play. That's the latest Elm Park fitness news as Reading prepared to take on Darlington on Saturday. Friday returned to his club today for the first time since last weekend's disastrous home 3–0 defeat by Barnsley. He has been in bed all week suffering from flu and bronchitis but now he is fighting to get fully fit again by Saturday.

JOHN MURRAY: On Friday mornings Robin would ask me to give him a lift to this house, just outside town. So we'd get there and I would wait outside watching all these people coming and going, not knowing what was going on. When Robin would finally come out he would have spent all his wages. He never had a penny.

SYD SIMMONDS: If he didn't have a game on in the week we'd probably – especially in warmish weather – go and drink all day, and go to a club later on. But from Thursday lunchtimes onwards he wouldn't drink. I'm a builder so I used to go to work most days. One night I came home and on the coffee table was a big dinner plate with an acid tab on it. He said, 'I've got a big treat for us tonight.' I said, 'Nah, I'm not doing that, we'll be jumping out the windows.' 'We'll be all right,' he said, 'just do half each.' I was a little nervous but to Robin that was just a joke.

Reading Evening Post, 1 November 1974
Reading 3 Darlington 0
. . . Reading manager Charlie Hurley said after his team's first win in six matches at Elm Park on Saturday: 'I think we have turned the

corner. Confidence was the key and this result will do the world of good for my players.'

Reading Evening Post, 6 November 1974
Hartlepool 2 Reading 3
. . . In the first half Reading looked like struggling no-hopers. In the second half they looked like a promotion team. Three minutes from the end Robin Friday, who had been knocked out during the second half, rammed home a brilliant through-ball from Gordon Cumming.

Division Four, 8 November 1974
1. Mansfield
2. Shrewsbury
3. Rotherham
4. Chester
5. Reading

Reading Evening Post, 8 November 1974
Workington 2 Reading 1
. . . Reading boss Charlie Hurley found out last night what a crazy mixed-up game football can be. On Wednesday Hurley had seen his team climb back into the title race with a magnificent 3–2 win at Hartlepool. Last night it all went wrong again. Upfront it was a disappointing night for the deadly duo Friday and Habbin, who were snuffed out by the Workington defence.

Division One, 9 November 1974
1. Manchester City
2. Liverpool
3. Everton

Reading Evening Post, 14 November 1974
Reading striker Robin Friday's showdown with the FA Disciplinary Committee has been rearranged for next Monday morning. Friday's

personal hearing goes on at the Association's headquarters in Lancaster Gate, London, an FA spokesman announced today. This is the case that was due to be held on 28 October but was called off when the player went down with flu.

Reading Evening Post, 16 November 1974
Reading 1 Bradford City 1
Friday scores a penalty.

Reading Evening Post, 18 November 1974
. . . Reading strikers Robin Friday and Dick Habbin were both in London today for hearings which could affect their futures. Friday faced more of a problem staving off a two-match suspension when he appeared before an FA disciplinary committee. He appealed to the FA against a booking by referee Len Burden at Broadstone, Dorset, for a foul on Southport goalkeeper Derek Edmunds. If it goes against him, Friday will be suspended for two games, probably from next Monday.

Tuesday Night TV, 19 November 1974
BBC1: *John Craven's Newsround, Mission: Impossible, Film 74*
ITV: *Wrestling, Mother Makes Five, Crossroads*

Reading Evening Post, 19 November 1974
. . . Robin Friday has been banned for two games. Charlie Hurley said, 'It might not prove such a bad thing after all. Robin had been playing under this 12-point cloud and I think it has affected his game slightly. But he will come back with a clean sheet and without any pressures on him.'

Friday will miss the Fourth Division matches against Doncaster Rovers and Lincoln the following week.

Reading Evening Post, 23 November 1974
Swindon 4 Reading 0
. . . Reading crashed out of the FA Cup today as Third Division
Swindon turned on a commanding performance.

CHARLIE HURLEY: Robin was the most honest player we had on
the pitch. As you know, he had asthma. One day he was playing
and he had an attack on the pitch. We quickly took him off and
into the dugout which was so low nobody could see in. We put
an overcoat over his head and got his inhaler out. 'How're you
doing, kid?' I asked. 'All right, boss, I'm getting better.' Suddenly
he relaxed and said, 'You've only got ten men out there, boss. Put
a sub on.' He was a real team player.

Reading Evening Post, 25 November 1974
Robin Friday was forced to leave the field during Reading's FA Cup
defeat at Swindon on Saturday. He is to undergo x-rays on his chest.
The Reading striker saw a doctor at the weekend and is believed to
have a chest infection. 'We hope the hospital will be able to clear up
the matter,' said manager Charlie Hurley today. 'Robin was in a bad
way on Saturday, he just couldn't breathe properly. He came off after
five minutes for an inhaler but that didn't do him much good. He was
coughing and when he came off for good I thought he was dying. He
is of course suspended from today and I have told him he has two
weeks to get himself fully fit. It seems that Friday wasn't too well on
Friday night, but the boy didn't tell me. The trouble is he was so
keen to play, but had he told me he wasn't too good I would have
thought twice about playing him.'

Reading Evening Post, 30 November 1974
Reading 2 Doncaster 0
. . . Stan Bowles, the controversial 24-year-old Queens Park Rangers
striker, has said that if he doesn't get the go-ahead for a transfer
later this week he is likely to switch to his old club, Manchester

City. When City's manager Tony Book heard of the transfer request put in by Bowles, he said, 'We are unlikely to be interested in the news.'

Reading Evening Post, 1 December 1974
Lincoln 1 Reading 1

Reading Evening Post, 6 December 1974
. . . Average weekly wage: £50 a week.
Average price of house in the Reading area: £15,000

Reading Evening Post, 13 December 1974
. . . Stan Bowles has been dropped by QPR for the home game against Sheffield United. Explaining his decision manager Dave Sexton said, 'It is extremely important that everyone who plays has got the club's interests at heart.'

MAURICE EVANS, READING COACH: Robin had great ability but he had so many things against him as well. He obviously was a bad athlete because of the way he lived. He had no pace but he had eyes in the back of his head. He could see things, he could control the ball and he had great confidence in himself – great confidence. And, basically, he was a smashing lad who was easily led by stupid people who got hold of him and he went their way rather than the way most people would go. That was sad, really, because he had so much talent.

ROD LEWINGTON: Everyone would talk to him about his lifestyle. If you got him just after he had finished training or if it was his day off and he was sitting indoors just listening to his records, you could talk logically to him. He would say, 'Yeah, I should do this or I should do that.' But he never had the willpower to do it because he was so easily led. The guys he hung out with they were all working but they all worked straight hours so they were always available. If they went down the pub they'd take him with them – that's how it was.

SYD SIMMONDS: He wasn't a heavy drinker. If you went and talked to the man in the street and asked about Robin they'd say, 'Brilliant footballer but always on the piss.' I probably drank more than him and I was a driver. And that stuff about him drinking before a game? Complete fantasy. Never. He did miss training on a Monday quite often, though. Charlie would come round to the flat and knock on the door at ten on a Monday morning and Robin would say he couldn't make it. He might have a hangover, he might have a bird in there, and they used to let him get away with it. Everyone else had to train but if Robin said, 'No, I'm not coming' then he wouldn't go and that was the end of it.

MAURICE EVANS: There was a load of rubbish spoken about his drinking before a game. He definitely did not. For one thing, Charlie would never have allowed it. After a game, sure, straight in. And maybe on a Friday night because Robin wasn't bothered about things like that. He'd say, 'I'm as fit as the rest of them.' He was never worried about fitness.

CHARLIE HURLEY: It was a lot of crap. I used to go up to him and put my arm around his shoulders and sniff. Robin would say, 'You caught me once but no more.' I'd tell him, 'Look, as much as I love you, kid, I am not taking the rap for you being pissed before a game.' I told him, 'If at all possible, try never to drink two days before a game.' But I think that might have been asking a lot of him.

ALF FRIDAY: He didn't bother about the booze. People get some stupid ideas in their heads. Robin was never a drinker. I know where they might get that story. Like the time someone let us down with a lift. We had to get the train from Paddington so we strolled out of Reading station and we didn't get a cab. We're walking up the road and we bump into David Dibben. We're strolling up – we didn't realise the time – and David came up and said, 'What are you doing? Charlie is going mad in there.' It was about twenty to three. And we're just strolling around. So you might glean something from that but Robin was never a drinker.

Reading Evening Post, 14 December 1974
Southport 2 Reading 0

Reading Evening Post, 18 December 1974
. . . Queen's Park Rangers have agreed to take Stan Bowles off the transfer list . . .

Reading Evening Post, 19 December 1974
. . . Reading are down to just 11 match-fit professionals for Saturday's game against Swansea City. The three men who won't be playing are Friday, Carnaby and Heztke. Friday still hasn't shaken off his chest complaint and has been in hospital this week for more tests and x-rays, while Heztke, who has been out for six weeks, is now sidelined by a thigh strain following his ankle injury.

Reading Evening Post, 21 December 1974
Reading 1 Swansea 2

Reading Evening Post, 28 December 1974
Reading 1 Stockport 3
. . . The game had been in progress for only 15 seconds when Friday was spoken to by the referee for a foul on Jim McNabb, the Stockport skipper and a former Sunderland colleague of Charlie Hurley's

. . . After a heated Stockport protest Friday coolly sent the keeper the wrong way to make it 2–1 with his twelfth goal of the season.

Reading manager Charlie Hurley said after the game, 'That was the worst defensive display I've ever seen,' and when asked if there had been any addition to the team's long injury list he replied, 'Yes, me, I was very hurt. For the first time since I came to the club I was really hurt by some things that happened in the game.' Hurley went on to use such words as, 'disgusting', 'appalling', and 'disgraceful' to describe various aspects of his team's performance. He is clearly now resigned to the fact that some of the side which has won only one of their eight games and three of their last 15 want to see someone else in his job. Once again some of the Reading team were put to shame by Robin Friday playing his first game for six weeks. It's a pity they can't find a player with his skill, spirit, bravery and above all enthusiasm for every position.

1975: The Getting of High

Reading Evening Post, 2 January 1975
. . . George Best arrested for drink driving . . .

Reading Evening Post, 6 January 1975
Crewe 1 Reading 0
. . . This is now Reading's fourth defeat on the trot and they have slumped to 12th place in Division Four, only three points clear of the bottom four.

Reading Evening Post, 11 January 1975
Reading 1 Lincoln City 0

DAVID DOWNS, READING FC HISTORIAN: Robin didn't socialise with the other players. His mates were all back in London and he had a very close-knit family who would come and watch him play at Reading. At every home game you would always see Robin's dad and his mum and his grandad. Apparently there was one game with Lincoln where Robin got some very hard tackles from a Lincoln player and those three were waiting outside the Lincoln dressing-room afterwards. Some of these stories may be apocryphal but I think there's a lot of truth in this general pattern of behaviour.

Reading Evening Post, 18 January 1975
Doncaster Rovers 1 Reading 1

Reading Evening Post, 25 January 1975
Brentford 0 Reading 0

Reading Evening Post, 26 January 1975
. . . Maggie Thatcher is going to challenge Ted Heath for the leadership of the Conservative Party . . .

Reading Evening Post, 30 January 1975
. . . The Reading Rock Festival has been given permission to carry on until 1977.

Reading Evening Post, 3 February 1975
Reading 3 Workington 0
. . . Maurice Evans reported the team's best win for three months. After only five goals in eight games came the luxury of three in one . . . including two in five minutes . . . the last of which alone was worth the price of a season-ticket . . . . Friday's goal, Reading's 50th of the season, in his own 50th first-team game, owed as much to foolhardiness as courage . . . Diving full length barely a foot off the ground, Friday risked life and limb to head home a truly memorable goal . . . True to form, he had to spoil things for himself by getting booked three minutes later . . . One could not help feeling slight sympathy on this occasion for his retaliation for the umpteenth bad foul from behind.

ALF FRIDAY: They all seemed like good games to me. I suppose when you are involved with someone you tend only to watch them. I saw him score a goal when he headed the ball full length and the ball was about an inch off the ground. That was a brilliant goal. The old man said to me, 'Fuck me, I don't know how he got to it.' His chest was more or less scraping the ground. I don't know how he got to it, it was that low.

Reading Evening Post, 5 February 1975
. . . A hectic 'Stop Maggie' movement is building up in the Tory Party today as Margaret Thatcher's bandwagon threatened to become unstoppable . . .

Reading Evening Post, 8 February 1975
Darlington 0 Reading 1
. . . The Darlington keeper did well to clear from Robin Friday and block a close-range volley from Lenarduzzi . . .

Reading Evening Post, 11 February 1975
Muhammad Ali is due to fight Chuck Wepner on 24 March and he has vowed not to hit him in the face during the World Heavyweight challenge . . .
. . . Maggie Thatcher becomes the first woman to head a British political party . . .

Division One, 15 February 1975
1. Stoke
2. Everton
3. Burnley

Reading Evening Post, 17 February 1975
Reading 1 Brentford 0

Reading Evening Post, 24 February 1975
Bradford 1 Reading 3
. . . Cock-a-hoop after four wins on the trot . . . Reading field an unchanged side for tonight's Fourth Division game against Hartlepool . . . The Reading side have the boost of knowing a win tonight would put them back within chance of promotion.
. . . MPs are worried that Margaret Thatcher possesses a right-wing streak and will take the Conservative Party further to the right.

Reading Evening Post, 24 February 1975

Reading 0 Hartlepool 0

. . . There were two losers in this game, football and the fans who paid to get in to see it. If every team used the tactics Hartlepool used, football would be dead within five years . . .

CHARLIE HURLEY: One of the reasons that Robin and I got on so well is because he knew that if he asked me a question he got a one hundred per cent honest answer. After a match he would ask me, 'How was I?' Because Robin loved to talk. I'd say, 'You were real crap.' He'd say, 'But I was better than so-and-so.' I said, 'We're not talking about so-and-so. Don't ever let your yardstick compare with his. Your yardstick as a player is very high and you've got to keep your standards high.' He'd look at me and say, 'I didn't think of it like that, boss.' He was very streetwise but he probably wondered when it came to a yardstick what I was talking about. Nevertheless, from then on, he used to say, 'You've taught me and you're right. I am in a different class. Even when I play badly I'm better than them playing well.' I said, 'Now you've got the yardstick right.'

But he was very hard work. I think you had to be an Irishman to look after Robin. You could never get it right but you could get it the best you were ever going to get it.

Reading Evening Post, 28 February 1975

. . . Joe Bugner agrees to fight Muhammad Ali . . .

DAVID DOWNS: To be honest, until Robin arrived Reading were a very mundane club. Win at home, lose away and never do anything spectacular. He really transformed that image almost on his own. He had a huge cult following. Lots of people went to Reading just to watch Robin and that lasted as long as he was there. He put a lot of people on the gate.

CHARLIE HURLEY: When a player like Robin arrives, the team all start realising that 'This guy has come from nowhere and he's better than me. Are there any more like him?' Actually, if there were, you'd have to have about 20 of them because you could never get them all to turn up!

Reading Evening Post, 28 February 1975
Northampton 0 Reading 3
. . . Battered, bruised and frustrated by Hartlepool just four days before, Reading again deployed their extraordinary new spirit last night . . . chalking up their biggest away win for four years . . . Friday himself got a knock and was replaced by Barry Wagstaff for the last 12 minutes, that's the first time I've seen him substituted.

Reading Evening Post, 6 March 1975
. . . To add to Hurley's problems, members of his team like Robin Friday and John Murray have missed some training this week because of injuries . . . Friday of course missed the last few minutes of the 3–0 win at Northampton . . .

Reading Evening Post, 10 March 1975
Reading 2 Chester 1
Now the race is on. Rip-roaring Reading blasted themselves well and truly into a Fourth Division promotion race with a stirring victory over Chester . . . Friday, like Cumming, ran himself to a state of exhaustion and only a courageous save by Grenville Millington denied him a late goal . . .
. . . George Best has been charged with bringing the game into disrepute after writing an autobiography with Michael Parkinson . . .

Reading Evening Post, 19 March 1975
Cambridge 1 Reading 0

DAVID DOWNS: When they played Cambridge Robin and Brendan Batson had a dust-up. Ron Atkinson was then the manager of Cambridge and he allegedly told Batson to break Robin legs. Anyway, Friday walked off with Batson at the end of the game and they shook hands. Then Robin said to him: 'Well played and no offence, mate. I've got nothing against blacks. After all, I am married to one.' I don't think Batson knew what to make of that.

Reading Evening Post, 24 March 1975
Reading 1 Scunthorpe 1
Reading's top scorer Robin Friday does not face another suspension after being booked in Saturday's 1–1 draw with Scunthorpe . . . Friday escapes a ban because his booking against Hartlepool only rated two disciplinary points and not the expected four . . .

Thursday Night TV, 24 March 1975
BBC 1: *Tomorrow's World, Top of the Pops, The Liver Birds*
ITV: *Born Free, Man About the House, The Sweeney*

ROD LEWINGTON: Sindlesham Mill was the in-place and Robin got banned from there every time. He used to go mad up there. His trick was to do the elephant. He'd pull his trouser-pockets inside out and undo his fly. So he'd have his pockets hanging out and his dick in the middle. That was doing the elephant.

Reading Evening Post, 29 March 1975
Swansea 1 Reading 2
. . . Robin Friday scored on 51 minutes and Taylor after 86 . . .

Reading Evening Post, 1 April 1975
Stockport 1 Reading 0
. . . The last straw for Reading . . . the home side did most of the

attacking throughout the match . . . Robin Friday was virtually left on his own isolated up front . . . One feels sorry for players such as Cumming, Leonard, Lenarduzzi, Friday and Death who have striven so hard in recent weeks.

MAURICE EVANS: Because the crowd loved him he wasn't afraid to fail, but you couldn't teach him anything. He was undisciplined as a team player. If you worked on set-plays and you said, 'When the ball comes here I want you to attack it,' as soon as he walked out onto the pitch it was gone and forgotten. He would go where he wanted to go. You couldn't work on anything with him to improve him. The only thing that I tried to do was improve his fitness – and he obviously didn't like that. He would play with the ball all day. Give him a ball and he loved it. But make him do some running and he hated it, detested it, thought it was a terrible waste of time. So what we did was to get him involved in five-a-side. That's what he loved. Players learn from each other and Robin was so good at that type of thing that you hoped the other players would pick up from him. And I'm sure they did.

Reading Evening Post, 3 April 1975
Reading 3 Exeter 0
Reading cruised to their most comfortable win of the season . . . Friday had what can only be described as a typical game . . . He received a knock straight from the kick-off but got up to throw himself head-first into another impressive performance . . . Robin's couple last night now makes him our club's leading scorer, his total of 17 being one more than Dick Habbin . . .

Reading Evening Post, 7 April 1975
Barnsley 2 Reading 0
. . . Reading paid dearly for a below-par performance . . . Charlie Hurley described referee George Knowles' handling of the Barnsley v Reading game as disgraceful. He said that the penalty decision was

the worst he had ever seen. 'We give them one goal to start and then the ref gives them another to consolidate – what chance have you got? We just didn't play well at all. You wouldn't have thought it was the same team.'

Reading Evening Post, 8 April 1975
. . . Reading Football Club is to refuse hooligans entry to the ground as the latest move in the fight against vandalism . . .

* * *

SYD SIMMONDS: He would spend a hundred quid on a pair of boots. He was mad for these crocodile boots. He would go and get them made in the King's Road somewhere and he'd only ever wear jeans. He never wore a blazer or trousers. All the others had to wear the club blazer and grey trousers. But Robin didn't. They used to come out of the dressing-room after the game and everyone would have all their hair blowdried and he'd come out with his hair all dripping wet and uncombed.

JOHN MURRAY: We were coming back on the train from a cup match in the North-east and West Ham were also travelling back. Steve Death used to be at West Ham so, after we'd eaten, a few of us went to the buffet car for a drink. Frank Lampard was there, with Clyde Best, Pat Holland and a few others. So we were all standing round having a chat when suddenly the carriage door goes bang, everyone turns around and there's Robin – long straggly hair, leather coat, black T-shirt and jeans. He says, 'Here, Minty, get us a fucking drink, will ya?' One of the West Ham players said, 'Fucking supporters, they get everywhere.' Deathy leant over and said, 'Actually, that's our centre-forward.'

Reading Evening Post, 11 April 1975
Reading 2 Rochdale 1

. . . Dull it was last night for PC Brian Miller until the unlikely lumbering shape of Robin Friday stepped into his life . . . Man Friday, overjoyed by his last-minute goal against Rochdale, was ready to kiss anyone . . . 'The policeman looked so cold and fed up standing there that I decided to cheer him up a bit' . . . 'You can tell Robin Friday that I didn't know he cared,' Miller said . . . Needing to win all their last six games to have any chance of promotion, Reading made terribly hard work of taking two points . . .

CHARLIE HURLEY: The next day in the paper there was a cartoon showing a queue of coppers waiting for Robin to give them a kiss. You don't have players like that these days.

JOHN MURRAY: The funny thing about it was that afterwards in the dressing-room Robin said he wished that he hadn't done it because he hated coppers so much.

Reading Evening Post, 14 April 1975
Torquay United 0 Reading 2
. . . Apart from Murray's goal, Saturday's game was memorable only for the complete lack of football played and the fact that the ref turned up five minutes late . . .

Reading Evening Post, 16 April 1975
Newport County 2 Reading 2
. . . This was a farcical game of four goals, four bookings and precious little football . . .

Reading Evening Post, 21 April 1975
Shrewsbury Town 2 Reading 0
. . . Reading manager Charlie Hurley admitted today, 'I know I was in the wrong shouting on to the pitch,' but, he added, 'I just can't understand why the ref sent me off' . . . Hurley now faces the possibility of being banned from the touchline, a similar

punishment handed out to the Crystal Palace manager, Malcolm Allison . . .

Reading Evening Post, 24 April 1975
Reading 1 Rotherham 1
. . . Robin Friday equalised Rotherham's tenth-minute goal . . . To lose Friday would be disaster of epic proportions but that could be a distinct possibility in the close season . . . His superb display last night could not have failed to impress Plymouth manager Tony Waiters who might have to move fast to pip Sheffield United who appear to be considering an offer that Reading will not be able to refuse . . . Friday's 55th-minute winner gave Reading the point they deserved . . .

Reading Evening Post, 28 April 1975
Reading 1 Mansfield 1
. . . Mansfield could do nothing about Friday's 25th-minute goal which put Reading in front . . .

JOHN MURRAY: Charlie Hurley was having a go at me for always finishing the cross-country runs last. There were four of us – myself, Robin, Steve Death and Brian Bromley – who always came last. It wasn't suprising. We'd be at the back running way behind everyone else and Deathy would say, 'Hang on, hang on, let's have a fag.' Then he'd reach down into his sock and pull out a packet of Park Drive and light up. So we'd stroll along like that and that was our pre-season training. Anyway, Charlie's getting real annoyed at me about this so one time I think, 'Right, I'm going to prove you wrong.' Off we go and I break away from Robin and keep going. After a while I look back. No one there. It's a red-hot day but I keep going. Look back again. No one there. Suddenly, a lorry carrying some scaffolding comes round the corner and, sure enough, who's on the back of it going, 'Fuck off, Minty, you wanker,' and hurling bits of scaffolding so that I have to jump in a ditch on the side of the road. I eventually get back to the ground and Charlie Hurley takes me to one side and shouts at me: 'I thought you said you were going to make an effort. Even fucking Robin beat you today.'

CHARLIE HURLEY: Robin was the belle of the ball as far as football in Reading goes. They loved him. He was such a good-looking boy. He had a lovely open face and he couldn't lie to you. Every time he told a porkie I knew straightaway. I'd say, 'Now, Robin, you've got the wrong face for lying.' He'd say, 'Okay then, boss, this is what really happened.'

ROD LEWINGTON: The funny thing about going out for a drink with Robin was that he was banned from so many places. He must have been banned from the Boar's Head about ten times. There was one time we walked in and the landlord said, 'Robin, you're banned. Out!' 'But Dick, all I want is a drink.' 'Out!' 'Come on, Dick, just a swift pint.' 'Robin, out!' So Robin walks out. Suddenly the window shoots open and Robin sticks his head in and shouts, 'I didn't want to drink in your poxy pub anyway!' The landlord was on the floor with laughter after Robin did that.

CHARLIE HURLEY: I always remember that one day some money was stolen. So I interviewed all the players in alphabetical order. I'm very good at knowing if people are lying. If you look at people's eyes you can always tell. You do get nervous people but I knew that. Robin comes in. Straightaway he says, 'You think I did it, don't you?' I said, 'Robin, the fact that you are talking like that is going to make other people inclined to think that you did. I know you didn't do it. I'd bet on all the players down there that you are the one that didn't do it.' He was a rough diamond and he was always on the earhole for money but he would never have stolen from the people he knew.

MAURICE EVANS: Charlie Hurley was brilliant with Robin. Charlie really handled him better than anyone could ever have done. He was very protective of Robin.

DAVID DOWNS: I thought Robin was a very generous person. He would always sign autographs. He would stay there signing autographs for kids all day. I was taking a party of schoolchildren to the central swimming-pool in Reading. The kids were all eight or nine and Robin was coming the other way. I said, 'Hello, Robin,' and he said, 'All right, you old fucker,' in front of all these eight-year-old kids. He didn't mean any harm by it. That was just his way and if any of those kids had asked for his autograph he would have stopped and signed them all day. You accepted him for what he was.

CHARLIE HURLEY: Robin was a revelation to us. We were always a good team but we never had quite enough class to get up. We were always in the hunt, always in the top eight. But Robin was the one who made it, who turned it around for us.

DAVID DOWNS: I think all players respected him for what he did as a team member. I should think that the person who would be closest to understanding him would be Eamon Dunphy because he had the intellectual nous to allow for Robin Friday's extremes.

EAMON DUNPHY, READING FC PLAYER: Morale at the club was poor before I got there. Charlie Hurley brought me there for a specific reason, which was to show some leadership and get promotion. Before I joined Reading in 1975 I had vaguely heard that Robin was a good player. My first impression was that I liked him, that he was wild but his lifestyle was not what we needed. As a professional player he was very undisciplined. He had talent all right, and a lot of it. I had come from a disciplined set-up at Millwall so that's why I felt like that. But I liked him. I liked him a lot. I shared a lot of his liking for a few drinks.

SYD SIMMONDS: We used to go to the Top Rank some Saturdays. There was John Murray, Gary Peters, Eamon Dunphy – all footballers – me and Mick O'Donnell. Robin and Gary used to hold hands on the top of the balcony and jump down into the club. The balcony was 15, 20 foot up and they'd jump down. Both were professional footballers. Crazy.

EAMON DUNPHY: We made a deal at the start of the season that if he and Minty [John Murray] got their act together and we did the business on the pitch, we would go and have a bit of fun afterwards – whereas they were inclined to have a bit of fun beforehand. Robin did train hard. He had all the qualities required and more, but what he needed was to hear someone he respected say, 'I can play as hard as you but let's do the business first.'

Reading Evening Post, 16 August 1975
Reading 2 Rochdale 0

Reading Evening Post, 23 August 1975
Crewe 3 Reading 3

DAVID DOWNS: I remember going to a game at Crewe that Robin played in right at the start of the 1975–76 season. Robin arrived shortly before the kick-off having travelled all across London on the tube and then up on the train. For this game at Crewe he arrived wearing a scruffy old jacket and a T-shirt and when he took his jacket off in the bar afterwards, I'll never forget that on the back of the T-shirt there was a big long red arrow pointing all the way down to his bottom and at the top was a sign saying, '2000 VOLTS'.

The chairman of the club at the time was a man called Frank Waller. I wouldn't say that he knew a lot about football – he knew some of the phrases – but he was good for the club. Reading had been losing this game 3–1 and had come back to draw 3–3. Afterwards, Waller was in the bar saying, 'I thought we showed a lot of character coming back to score twice.' Robin was standing next to him and said, 'It's like me, Chairman, I showed a lot of character over the Forbury Gardens yesterday.' Apparently, this is where he had been with his girlfriend after training. The phrase he then used was, 'In and out like a fiddler's elbow, I was,' but I think that was probably lost on the chairman, who was about 70 at this stage.

Reading Evening Post, 30 August 1975
Reading 1 Southport 0

Reading Evening Post, 6 September 1975
Lincoln 3 Reading 1

Reading Evening Post, 13 September 1975
Reading 3 Watford 0
. . . Robin Friday hammered an unstoppable shot in the roof of the net from outside the box . . . it was his fourth goal of the season . . . His face looks as though it had been trampled on by a rugby squad and that was before the game. Friday's explanation: 'Me missus hit me with a can of beans.'

SYD SIMMONDS: All I'll say is that there would be girls knocking on the flat door at two or three in the morning.

Reading Evening Post, 20 September 1975
Workington 0 Reading 2
Robin Friday grabbed a goal on Saturday to sink Workington . . . he
maintained his record of scoring in every away game this season and
put the result beyond doubt.

Reading Evening Post, 23 September 1975
Hartlepool 2 Reading 4
Reading manager Charlie Hurley summed it up perfectly when he
said about his team's second away win in three days, 'We were
magic.' This victory, Reading's fourth in succession, puts them a
point clear at the top of the Fourth Division . . .

Reading Evening Post, 27 September 1975
. . . Reading have the perfect chance to prove to the fans that their
early form is no flash in the pan. The big point of interest in today's
game is the clash between Reading's top scorer Robin Friday and
former Elm Park centre-half Stuart Morgan, who joined Bournemouth last season from Colchester. It's a real battle of the giants
which could keep the referee extremely busy. Friday won the
admiration of his team-mates when he received a fearful kicking at
Hartlepool and made no move to retaliate for the first time in his
career.

Reading Evening Post, 29 September 1975
Reading 2 Bournemouth 1
Friday sent off . . . Five more booked . . . Reading grabbed two points
out of the fire at Elm Park. The heroes were two-goal Dunphy and
the villain was Robin Friday who was sent off . . . In the 22nd minute
Friday got in a superb diving header which put the ball just inches
past the post . . .

. . . Friday stupidly aimed a punch at Payne and both he and the
Bournemouth number 2 were cautioned . . . Two minutes later the
referee took a fourth name, that of former Reading defender Stuart

Morgan, for tripping Friday. Morgan seemed to be the innocent party as Friday apparently took a dive on this occasion. Nil–nil at half time . . .

Dunphy slammed his first goal for the club after a brilliant dribble by Robin Friday . . . With 11 minutes remaining, Friday finally launched one assault too many on the volatile Morgan and was quite rightly sent off. Nothing, it seems, can curb Friday's petulance although in the very last game at Hartlepool he was mercilessly hacked throughout the match without a hint of retaliation. His actions on Saturday were, of course, entirely indefensible. But it is worth noting that his team-mates and manager think he's far more sinned against than sinned. Far from putting his team at a disadvantage, however, being outnumbered had the best possible effect, for Friday's dismissal was the signal for the home side to throw everything before them . . .

MAURICE EVANS: The crowd loved Robin – absolutely adored him. He used to do a lap of honour when he scored a goal. They really loved him. He had something about him – I don't know how you could describe it – but he would do things that other players couldn't do. For instance, the ball was up the other end of the field and there is a player laid on the ground and Charlie Hurley said to me, 'I bet that was Robin,' and it was. The fella's laid out in the other penalty area and the ball's up the other end. Charlie got him at half-time and he said, 'What the fuck are you doing?' Robin said, 'Well, he called me a gypsy.' There were things like that happening all the time because he had long hair and he wore an earring which was very unusual for the time.

Reading Evening Post, 31 September 1975
. . . Reading's leading striker Robin Friday, sent off against Bournemouth at Elm Park on Saturday, will not have to serve an automatic ban. Friday, the other Reading players and their supporters, thought the long-haired striker would be suspended for one or two games

. . . Having been booked on one previous occasion already this season, Friday must be close to the 20 points needed for his case to come before the FA Disciplinary Committee and he would then get a three-match ban . . . It now remains to be seen if Hurley will discipline Friday himself . . . Hurley refused to criticise Robin after his dismissal: 'Robin's a great lad,' he said. But under the new misconduct code, the onus is on clubs to control their own players. Any club whose players reach 100 points will have to face the FA and the possibility of a heavy fine.

JOHN MURRAY: We were sitting in a café one time and there were all these taxi-drivers talking about prison. I didn't know anything about Tony, Robin's brother [being in prison], and one of them started saying that if you were put inside you deserved it because you shouldn't be that stupid. Next thing I know Robin has leapt up and he's on this guy, jabbing him in the face with a fork. It was unbelievable. He snapped so quickly.

CHARLIE HURLEY: The thing is, when you have a player like Robin it's hard work because you don't know what's happening when you're not there. He used to come in on a Monday or a Tuesday with a black eye – and he didn't get it playing on the Saturday. He'd say to me he got it in a scrap or when he was drunk. I'd say, 'Look, if I don't ask you, I don't have to listen to you. I'll just assume you walked into a door.' He did have a couple of scrapes with the police but I knew the law. I was always ahead of the game. I always made sure that the chief constable came to games and was always invited. I'd say to him, 'If there's any trouble let me know about it. But the thing is, a lot of the coppers were Robin Friday fans.'

Reading Evening Post, 1 October 1975
. . . Muhammad Ali beat Joe Frasier in the Thriller in Manila in 14 savage rounds and said that instincts saved him from death . . .

CHARLIE HURLEY: Jimmy Wallbanks was the old trainer. One day
he was massaging Robin – he always smoked when he was
massaging. He was a great old boy, a great talker. You used to get
a lot of physios who would take your mind off your injury by
being a comic. Jimmy is massaging Robin one day and he's
smoking and the hot ash keeps falling onto Robin's leg and
mixing with the oil. So Robin goes, 'Jim, you're dropping your
ash onto my leg.' Jimmy looked at him and, without missing a
beat, said, 'It's all part of the treatment, Robin.'

Reading Evening Post, 2 October 1975
Robin Friday has tasted the good and bad side of soccer in a week
which saw Reading stay top of Division Four and entertain First
Division QPR. Friday and QPR goalkeeper Phil Park received their
Man of the Match award from Elm Park physio Jimmy Wallbanks,
whose testimonial raised more than £4,000.

A few days earlier Friday had received his marching orders in the
home league clash against Bournemouth and that sending-off had
the soccer statisticians scratching their heads. Who, they
wondered, was the last Reading player to get his marching orders in
a home game? Well, the answer to that is that Friday broke a good
record going back to April '68 when fiery little full back John Chapel
was ordered off along with Oldham's Keith Bevinson.

Reading Evening Post, 6 October 1975
Scunthorpe 2 Reading 1
. . . Some players need to be more hungry in the box like Robin
Friday . . . It was Friday's goal which provided consolation after a left-
wing cross from Ray Hiron. It was Friday's sixth goal of the season,
keeping Reading's record of having scored in every league game and
the club as the highest scorers in all four divisions away from home
. . . Unfortunately, Friday's afternoon was spoiled by yet another
booking following a trip from behind. His only foul of the game . . .

By that time three other players should have had their names on the score-sheet . . .

Reading Evening Post, 11 October 1975
Reading go into this afternoon's game knowing that a victory and the two points will take them then back into third place in Division Four . . .

JOHN MURRAY: One Friday night there were two or three of us in this hotel room watching TV. I think Eamon Dunphy was there and so was Steve Death, the goalkeeper. Steve smoked so when they lit up these 'cigarettes' I didn't think anything of it. Next thing I know I'm going, 'This is a great film and what a lovely room we're in and look at the sky out there . . .'

Reading Evening Post, 13 October 1975
Bradford City 1 Reading 2
. . . Extra shooting practice will be ordered this week for Reading's players. Not only did they throw away many golden opportunities to improve their goal difference, but they wasted a chance of a scoreline that would frighten the life out of their opponents in the Fourth Division . . . Robin Friday had a good game despite constant hackings.

MAURICE EVANS: On the coach he was always fooling around, always. He couldn't keep still. He was always rattling around doing all sorts to the other players. He probably had only two or three close team-mates, and the rest of the team . . . well, it was a strange relationship. They thought he was a brilliant player but as a person they weren't too sure about him.

EAMON DUNPHY: I always had a good relationship with Robin and I can't ever remember getting angry with him because generally I thought he was great. We used to have a go at the silly straight fuckers. We were the rebels. I was always with the boys at the back of the bus. We used to have a lot of fun on the bus. We'd smoke a joint, pop some pills, have a real laugh. It was relatively harmless. The only thing with Robin was that you'd always have to say, 'Wait until we get a result and then you can do whatever you like.'

ROGER TITFORD, AUTHOR: One time they were travelling back from a game and Robin wanted to use the toilet. So they pulled the coach up by the cemetery and he and Dunphy, I think, got out. Robin then realised they were next to a cemetery so he leapt over the wall and came back with some stone angels. He was going to put them next to the chairman, Frank Waller, who was sleeping on the coach at the time.

CHARLIE HURLEY: He came back on the coach with these angels and I took him to one side and I said, 'Robin you must never ever desecrate a graveyard because whoever is down there will come and haunt you for the rest of your life.' He had these big eyes and they were getting bigger and bigger and I said it so seriously he went, 'All right, boss,' and put them back.

ALF FRIDAY: Robin never talked about the other players. That was the difference between him and them. In them days it was an unwritten rule. You didn't talk about each other. They never ever slagged one another off. I think it was a good thing.

Thursday Night TV, 16 October 1975
BBC 1: *The Wombles, Nationwide, Tomorrow's World, Top of the Pops, The Two Ronnies, Mastermind*
ITV: *Crossroads, Six Million Dollar Man, This Week,*

*Get Some In, Labour Party Broadcast, The Stars Look
Down, Orson Welles' Great Mysteries, Take Two, What
the Papers Say*

Reading Evening Post, 16 October 1975
Reading manager Charlie Hurley is strongly tipped to become the
new manager of Sheffield United. I understand he is favourite to take
over at Bramhall Lane from Ken Furphy who was sacked last year. A
former Eire international, Hurley has been in charge at Elm Park
since January '72. He felt at the time that he did not have enough
experience to become a Division One boss but now I fancy Hurley,
at the age of just 38, might have the confidence to jump at the
chance.

Reading Evening Post, 20 October 1975
Barnsley 4 Reading 2
. . . Reading's two goals in the 4–2 defeat came from the most and
least predictable sources – Robin Friday, of course, and Stewart
Henderson. It was Friday's seventh of the season . . . The big
number 9, Reading's star man, headed home from a cross at close
range after John Murray had flicked the ball up.

Reading Evening Post, 22 October 1975
Newport County 0 Reading 0
Eamon Dunphy had atrocious luck when a superb pass from Friday
bobbled just in front of him, causing him to volley over. Both
Whitham and Hiron failed by inches to turn Robin Friday crosses
into empty nets . . . Meanwhile, Steve Death didn't have one direct
shot to bother with . . . Once again, however, we were left to reflect
on a string of chances and what might have been.

Reading Evening Post, 21 October 1975
Reading 2 Huddersfield 0

. . . Reading's players launch a fierce attack on the Elm Park fans who jeered them throughout their 2–0 win over Huddersfield. The team are bitterly upset at what they consider unfair treatment by their own supporters. Several players were astonished when they heard the fans humming the death march on Saturday. Top scorer Robin Friday said, 'That crowd makes me sick. All the time they seemed to be picking on Gordon Cumming, but he's played consistently well all season.' But Cumming, who scored Reading's first goal, said, 'They don't upset me.' Midfielder Eamon Dunphy said, 'When they started humming the death march I have never heard anything like it in all my years of professional football. The key to the problem on Saturday was Huddersfield. They were the sort of side who would make any team look bad. They were extremely hard to beat but we had to keep on trying to play football.' Manager Charlie Hurley said, 'What I think of our fans is unprintable. I don't mind them shouting at me but I don't want them upsetting my players. People must realise that sometimes you have to sit until the 89th minute to get the winning goal. But if they want us to play kick and rush, that's the best way to invite defeat.'

Reading Evening Post, 26 October 1975
The Reading players' attack for the treatment they got from the home crowd on Saturday during the 2–0 win over Huddersfield has got the fans talking. Meanwhile, Charlie Hurley has asked me to point out the players did not mean to upset the hardcore 4,000 or so fans who have always supported them.

Reading Evening Post, 30 October 1975
HOW I WAS ARRESTED by Robin Friday
Reading football star Robin Friday told today of the nightclub incident which has led to him being charged with using obscene language. The 23-year-old top goal-scorer is to appear before magistrates at Newport, Gwent, on 17 November. Friday announced today that he would plead not guilty to the charge.

Speaking from the Elm Park ground shortly before a training session, Friday said, 'It was all a joke.' After the evening match Friday and a friend visited a nightclub. 'The incident happened as we were leaving the club at about 1.30 in the morning. I wasn't drunk or anything – I didn't get there until quite late because it was an evening match. One of my mates went over to the police outside and was messing about. All he did was give a Harvey Smith sign as a joke and they arrested him. I went over to see what was going on and they dragged me in. They said, "You can come along as well," and it wasn't until after they arrested me that I started swearing. I shall plead not guilty and I don't need a solicitor because I shall put my own case.' Friday, who was voted Player of the Year last season, said the court appearance will not affect his game: 'I appear at the court on the Monday and we play Torquay United on the Saturday but I'll have plenty of time to get to Newport.'

EAMON DUNPHY: When I was there he went missing now and again. But he didn't go missing in a big way. He had a good season and we started off well and we were there in the frame all season. So there were only a few lapses. Like, say, a Gazza or a George Best or a Paul McGrath, who was very much like that in his early years, there is no use acting the schoolmaster. You've got to be man about it. You've got to say, 'This guy does it on the pitch so you've got to be tolerant and manage the situation off the pitch.' I said to Robin, 'Okay, I know you've gone off the rails, you can make up for it on the pitch.' It's not the end of the world if there are a few breaches of discipline. What we wanted was a warrior and Robin certainly was a warrior.

Reading Evening Post, 3 November 1975
Doncaster Rovers 1 Reading 1
In terms of their promotion prospects, Reading's 1–1 draw on Saturday was an excellent result. But in one way the afternoon was a disaster because now Robin Friday, star striker, faces a virtually

certain three-match suspension . . . He's the first player to reach 20 points in the new disciplinary court . . . Friday is, of course, a lot more than Reading's top scorer and best striker. He is the most vital cog in the team, and last week I understand Reading turned down a £60,000 bid from Cardiff City involving Welsh international Derek Shallis . . .

Reading Evening Post, 5 November 1975
Reading 1 Swansea 0
. . . Robin Friday turned in yet another outstanding game last night and so did quite a few others, particularly Gordon Cumming, Tommy Youlden and Jeff Barker against Exeter on Saturday . . .

Reading Evening Post, 7 November 1975
. . . It is exactly a year since Lord Lucan disappeared and there has been no sign of him as yet . . . Wigan is one of the towns which is currently the centre of an amazing musical phenomenon known, for want of a better title, as Northern Soul . . . For today's game against Exeter City this afternoon Reading will definitely keep an unchanged team including Robin Friday in his last game before facing an FA disciplinary committee . . .

Reading Evening Post, 8 November 1975
Reading 4 Exeter 3
Ray Hiron clinches seven-goal thriller . . . Transfer listed John Murray was the hero of Reading this afternoon. After twice being behind against Exeter, Reading staged a storming recovery. Robin Friday got the first . . . Friday, who also faces a two- or three-match suspension, was again booked.

Division One, 8 November 1975
1. West Ham
2. Derby County
3. QPR

Division Two, 8 November 1975
1. Sunderland
2. Bolton

Division Three, 8 November 1975
1. Crystal Palace
2. Hereford

Division Four, 8 November 1975
1. Northampton
2. Lincoln
3. Tranmere
4. Reading

Reading Evening Post, 11 November 1975
The skills of soccer idol George Best were back on show last night. The wayward genius pulled in a crowd of 8,000 as struggling Stockport drew with First Division Stoke . . . That was four times the size of Stockport's normal gate . . . Best, given a free transfer by United, has joined Stockport on a month's loan . . . His new club are the next visitors to Reading.

Reading Evening Post, 14 November 1975
. . . Brilliant striker Robin Friday made a plea for leniency to the FA today . . . Friday was asking for his suspension to be cut from three matches to two. He was appearing before the committee to make a personal appeal after reaching 20 points under the new disciplinary code . . .

. . . Charlie Hurley accompanied him to Lancaster Gate, London . . . Before the meeting Hurley said, 'Under the new system I don't even know if I will get a chance to speak on Robin's behalf. All I want is just to be able to say a few words in the hope that I can get the ban chopped from three to two. You may think that Robin has a bad record but there's plenty you can say in his defence. If I get the opportunity I will tell them that he is kicked right up in the air throughout every game he plays. He takes more stick than all the rest of my players put together . . . He is the only striker I have ever known who gets back to tackle all the time and that's why he's booked so often.'

. . . Robin has been booked nine times and sent off once in his two years with Reading but in fact that's an improvement . . . His record before he came to Reading was quite abominable. Friday was sent off *seven times* in amateur football before joining Reading . . . He reached 22 points after being booked against Southport . . .

Reading Evening Post, 12 November 1975
With star striker Robin Friday banned from the next three matches, the battle is on for the Reading number 9 shirt . . . Hurley said Vernon Stokes, chairman of the committee, really spelled it out for him. He told Hurley he had heard Friday was a great player and a great entertainer and he would have to curb his temper if he wanted to get anywhere . . . 'I told Mr Stokes that I had fined Robin and tried everything else I could think of short of not playing him. I am not sure I am going to do that . . . He's worth two players to me.'

EAMON DUNPHY: Reading is a funny old place and Robin was a Londoner. He was a very intelligent guy but he had a low boredom threshold and that was one of his problems. In football, when you're doing it right, there are a lot of periods of quiet and boredom – because you have to be bored to store up your adrenaline and strength. From Wednesday onwards you have to get your body right, get yourself together and find a way of having fun and relaxation without abusing yourself. And that was one of Robin's problems.

SYD SIMMONDS: He was happy-go-lucky. He didn't give a

monkey's about anything. He would get his wages on the Friday, blow the lot over the weekend, and be skint in the week.

MAURICE EVANS: He was a drinker and after a game he would go in the bar and because everyone loved him they all wanted to buy him a drink. It must have been hard for him but he couldn't overcome it. He went with it.

JOHN MURRAY: He used to have these boils on his knees – all over them, they were. He would never eat, you see. He'd sit down for a meal but more often than not he would throw his food back on the plate or at other people. Some of the lads would actually take him back to their homes just so he would have something inside him.

Reading Evening Post, 15 November 1975
Torquay United 0 Reading 0
Reading hung on for a point . . . clearly missing the suspended Robin Friday . . . Reading's next home game is 6 December against Stockport County and George Best. Or so we hope . . .

Reading Evening Post, 7 November 1975
Robin Friday is due to appear in front of magistrates in Newport, Gwent, charged with using obscene language. The 23-year-old striker was jailed after an incident in a nightclub following the away game at Newport County on 20 October. Friday says one of his friends left the club and gave a Harvey Smith sign to a group of police outside.

Reading Evening Post, 22 November 1975
Hendon 1 Reading 0
Not a lot to be said . . . Reading forwards need to have shooting practice this week.

Reading Evening Post, 28 November 1975
Hopes of George Best playing for Stockport this Saturday against Reading look remote ... Best will stick to his original agreement of playing only in home games.

Reading Evening Post, 5 December 1975
George Best will definitely not play for Stockport ... I am told that an agent of Best's approached Reading and asked them to guarantee him a share of the gate money to play ... When his request was met with an emphatic *no*, Best said he would not play. Of course, it would have been highly illegal if Reading had agreed to this request ... The possibility of Best playing at Reading still sold more centre-stand tickets than usual for tomorrow's game but more people will be pleased to see Robin Friday back in the Reading line-up than the rare chance to see Best in action ...

... QPR problem boy Stan Bowles has been axed from the championship side to meet Manchester City tomorrow ... Manager Dave Sexton is having talks with George Best ... QPR, whose attacking style would suit the Irishman, emerged as favourites over Celtic to sign the former United star.

> Singles released this week include 'Hello Nadine' by Mungo Jerry, 'Santa Claus is Coming to Town' by The Carpenters, 'Evil Woman' by ELO, 'Jingle Bell Funk' by The Funky Turkey, 'In For A Penny' by Slade, 'Baby The Rain Must Fall' by Jonathan King.

CHARLIE HURLEY: I remember Wolves phoned up about him. They were asking, 'Is he this? Is he that?' I said, 'Listen, Robin Friday is the best centre-forward in the Fourth Division. Now, whatever else he is, and he's not perfect, you and I both know that real talent like him doesn't come easy. It never does.'

JOHN MURRAY: One night one of the lads had a lass in his room and a couple of the others were outside the door. Bruce Stuckey was serenading this girl under the door. Then Robin came along and asked them what they were doing. They told him so Robin turned to the door, gave it a couple of Kung Fu kicks and the door came down. The manager was going mad. Later on we were in the bar and I asked where Our Man Friday was – that's what we called him. No one knew. They kept swans in the hotel grounds. Next thing the bar door opens and in comes Robin with a swan under his arm. That's right, *a swan.* I said, 'Robin, they'll call the police for that,' so he takes it back outside. Some of the things he did were funny but other times they were just mad.

Reading Evening Post, 8 December 1975
Reading 5 Stockport County 0
The game started in a flurry of heavy tackles . . . Two goals in two minutes by Robin Friday at the start of the second half put Reading firmly in control. Stockport had started well after the interval and two good clearances by Youlden had saved Reading's lead . . . Reading's second goal came after a mistake from Davies whose weak back-pass was intercepted by Hiron who crossed for Friday to fire into an open goal . . . In the very next attack Friday scored again, his tenth of the season. Stuckey made this goal with a fine run down the left which Hopkins could only parry and Friday arrived at the right time to plant the ball in the net . . . This was the signal for Reading to play some superb attacking football. Friday was quickly hacked down by Smith and veteran international Dunphy had to race across the field to restrain his team-mate and prevent him from taking his revenge . . . The incident persuaded Friday to put on shinpads for the very first time. Goal number four came after 74 minutes and had to be seen to be believed . . . Friday pushed the ball through the Stockport defence with the outside of his boot and turned his back

completely on play to disarm Stockport . . . At first it fooled his team-mates as well but they gathered their wits and Stuckey laid on the cross for Murray to score again with a diving header . . . Number five was Murray's hat-trick and Stuckey's hat-trick of assists. Despite two men snapping at his heels, Murray was the first to Stuckey's centre to convert . . . Usually at this time of year it all goes wrong but this time Reading's play is going from strength to strength. They have another game next week against Scunthorpe with a chance to equal the 1949 record of ten home wins on the trot.

CHARLIE HURLEY: Robin had loads of skill and was very, very brave. You rarely get these qualities in the Fourth Division. The one thing he lacked was a bit of pace. If he'd had pace they would never have got near him.

EAMON DUNPHY: Robin was desperately anxious to improve himself and play in a higher division. He could have but he had this reputation and in football they exaggerate your faults. I think Robin was a victim of that. But he was the making of that team.

CHARLIE HURLEY: Robin had great vision and he loved scoring goals – loved it. He would go deep, he'd go wide, he'd do anything to drag people out of position. He talked to centre-halves, upset them. At the first corner he would be right up against the goalkeeper. It was good tactics because for the rest of the game the goalie would be wondering, 'Where's that big guy?' He was never going to damage a goalkeeper but keepers like to think that they are going to go up like a budgie and pick everything out of the air without anyone going to go near them, and Robin just wouldn't let that happen. He upset a lot of goalkeepers and a lot of centre-halves and he took a good kicking for it. But I have never known a guy so hard who could always smile at the end of it.

Reading Evening Post, 15 December 1975
Reading 1 Scunthorpe 0
Reading's record-equalling ten consecutive Fourth Division home wins in their 1–0 victory over Scunthorpe on Saturday was their least convincing display at Elm Park this season . . . However, to play badly and still win is a sign of a good team . . .

Reading Evening Post, 20 December 1975
Tranmere Rovers 2 Reading 0
Reading's unbeaten run came to a sickening end at Prenton Park last night despite the fact that they played their best football of the season . . . Reading's best chance of an equaliser came five minutes before the interval when keeper Dick Johnson deflected Robin Friday's shot against the inside of the post.

Reading Evening Post, 24 December 1975
Reading manager Charlie Hurley has delayed the announcement of his side . . . The Reading boss has hinted that there will be at least one change and extra training on Christmas Day and he will probably wait until that session is over before naming his team. Ron Atkinson also has problems [at Cambridge] and may drop Bobby Shinton . . .

Reading Evening Post, 27 December 1975
Reading 1 Cambridge 0
Ray Hiron scored the only goal of the match for Reading against Cambridge. The match was watched by the biggest crowd at Elm Park this year, 7,783 . . .

Reading Evening Post, 29 December 1975
Malcolm Allison, television personality and manager of Crystal Palace, was charged earlier today with driving while unfit through drink.

Christmas Eve TV, 1975

BBC 1: *Jim'll Fix It, Walt Disney Presents, Dick Emery Show, Porridge, Christmas With Kojak, Andre Previn's Christmas Night*

BBC 2: *Carols From The Kings, Moving Picture Show, Christmas Opera, The Old Grey Whistle Test*

ITV: *Crossroads, This is Your Life, Coronation Street, Merry Christmas Fred Astaire, Six Million Dollar Man, Pope Paul*

Reading Evening Post, 29 December 1975

Brentford 2 Reading 2

Midfielder Bruce Stuckey will say thank you to the gods for his fluke last-gasp goal direct from a corner which saved Reading at Griffin Park . . . With 20 minutes to go and two goals down, Hurley threw caution to the wind . . . Gordon Cumming became the fourth Reading player to be sent off this season, along with Robin Friday and youngsters Adrian Cooper and Trevor Porter. Of the trio, only Friday was not automatically suspended because his dismissal was for persistent infringement . . .

1976: Abdication of a King

JOHN MURRAY: Liza was a good lass. She calmed him down. At first.

LIZA FRIDAY: I was born and educated in Reading and I went to university in Liverpool and did a degree in English. Then I returned to Reading and I was living in this house where when everything is shut you'd all go back there and it would be full of people until the morning. I can remember meeting Robin there. Robin always came across to everyone as a character because he was so outrageous, I think there was an attraction in him for both men and women. It was his ability at football combined with his outrageousness. He was always the one that people wanted to talk to. I suppose that is what it was for me. There was an instant attraction there. He was in the middle of separating from Maxine and I think it was on one of those occasions when everybody was back at the house that he asked me out.

Reading Evening Post, 5 January 1976
Reading 1 Northampton 0
. . . It's looking good, Reading. Yes, promotion on after 50 years without a move up. Reading Football Club are now in their most promising position for 50 years . . . Northampton barely created a clear-cut chance whereas Robin Friday had four good scoring opportunities within ten minutes of the start of the second half . . . Friday had another fine game.

New singles out this week, 10 January 1976
'I Could Dance All Night' by Archie Bell and the
    Drells, 'The Horse' by Cliff Noble.

Reading Evening Post, 12 January 1976
Reading 2 Southport 1
Reading players today were still trying to fathom out how goalkeeper Steve Death pulled off a sensational injury-time penalty save
. . . Elm Park today reacted in amazement to yesterday's FA match
committee recommendation that the kissing and the cuddling has
got to stop. Reading players and officials are all agreed that surely
there are far more important things in the game to worry about.
Club captain Gordon Cumming was adamant: 'There are no players
who kiss each other in this club. It's the most natural instinct of all
to congratulate a player who's scored a goal when you've worked
hard all week with them to achieve something on Saturday. All we
do here is to pat the scorer on the bum to congratulate him. This
recommendation is the last thing I would worry about. I would just
like to get a few more goals myself.' Manager Charlie Hurley's
comment on the committee's recommendation: 'It's the biggest joke
I've ever heard in my life. They seem to be suggesting that players
are homosexuals but in all my time in the game I've never heard of
one that is. To kiss a bloke who's scored a goal is a perfectly natural
reaction. I nearly kissed Steve Death when he saved that penalty at
Southport on Saturday.'

Division One, 12 January 1976
1. Manchester United
2. Leeds
3. Liverpool
4. Derby

Division Two, 12 January 1976
1. Sunderland
2. Bolton
3. Bristol

Division Three, 12 January 1976
1. Crystal Palace
2. Walsall
3. Brighton

Division Four, 12 January 1976
1. Lincoln
2. Northampton
3. Reading

Reading Evening Post, 19 January 1976

Reading 1 Workington 0

This game will not be remembered for its football. That's not surprising as there was hardly any played . . . Reading's frustration was complete when Workington's goalie brought off a superb save to keep out what looked like a glorious second from Robin Friday . . . In the last minute Friday was booked in an incident with Hislop.

CHARLIE HURLEY: I never put anything in the papers about him. I knew loads of things about Robin but nothing went in the press. The press used to say to me, 'I hear Robin is doing this or that.' I'd say, 'First of all, you're a reporter on Reading football club, this is promotion year and he's the top striker in the Division. He had a great game last Saturday. What's the problem? Because if you're stirring the shit about Robin, you will find it very difficult getting a pass and having anything to do with the club. And you need us, this is our year.' I took a chance. In life, if you can get in the driving seat, you get in there.

Reading Evening Post, 20 January 1976
. . . Stan Bowles could be heading for soccer's wilderness. Transfer-listed at his own request yesterday for the third time in the three and a half stormy years at Queens Park Rangers, the 26-year-old star who has taken the mantle as the game's most controversial player could have difficulty in finding a new club . . .

Reading Evening Post, 23 January 1976
Robin Friday made it a good Friday for Charlie Hurley when he walked into Elm Park this morning. It meant the club's extrovert striker is fit and able to play at Watford tomorrow. Friday has been confined to his home with a cold.

JOHN MURRAY: He'd do anything to play on a Saturday afternoon. Whatever the injury, he'd say, 'Fuck them, boss, I'll be all right.' See, I don't think he knew what to do if he didn't play on a Saturday afternoon.

LIZA FRIDAY: Robin came from a very close-knit family. There are lots of aunts and uncles and they all keep in touch with his parents. And his mother's father, who lived to quite a ripe old age, was a definite influence on Robin's football. I remember meeting him and he was a typical old Londoner. I think the grandfather and father spent a lot of time at the dog tracks. I didn't grow up in a particularly close-knit family unit but he did. I remember we used to get on the tube and go to his parents' house out of our heads. His mum ironed his shirts. We used to see an awful lot of them. They always had their annual holidays in Great Yarmouth in the same chalet every year. So he didn't come from a family where he would have needed to go off the rails. I think he was an average teenager from that area. I think it was a wild area. I remember him telling me about gangs.

Reading Evening Post, 26 January 1976
Watford 2 Reading 1
. . . Reading kept on the pressure and an intelligent first-time ball to
the near post by Henderson saw Rankin dive full length to fool
Friday. After this incident Friday was spoken to at some length by
the referee . . . The goal followed a long free-kick which Hiron
headed down inside the box for Friday to shoot on the turn and
drive his shot home just inside the far post. Watford equalised 60
seconds later . . .

Reading Evening Post, 6 February 1976
A move to get Reading to drop the annual rock festival was
withdrawn yesterday . . .

Reading Evening Post, 8 February 1976
Swansea 5 Reading 1
Reading players were left last night wondering if they had created
some sort of new record for soccer suicide . . . They managed to
score three own-goals . . . Charlie Hurley said, 'I have never seen
such an unbelievable game in my life. It was really a false scoreline.
Even John Charles, the Swansea coach, admitted they were
flattered by the result . . . Hiron went close with a glancing header
before setting up the consolation goal for Robin Friday in the 77th
minute. There was still time for Friday to produce two more
brilliant efforts to emphasise what might have been, although
Swansea were denied a sixth goal. At the end of the nightmare
only Friday, Stuckey and Youlden had reason to hold their heads up
high.

Reading Evening Post, 14 February 1976
Exeter City 4 Reading 1
Hurley's new plan misfires: Reading's well-rehearsed plans to make a
restricting 4-4-2 system and their intention of making a tight
defence first priority survived for exactly five minutes last night . . .

How much longer can they afford to play with Friday as a one-man forward-line?

Reading Evening Post, 16 February 1976
'There's no need to panic,' says Charlie Hurley.

Reading Evening Post, 17 February 1976
Reading manager Charlie Hurley dropped nine of his first-team players to the reserves. Hurley named a squad of 13 for the game in this afternoon's football combinations fixture including Steve Death, Gordon Cumming, Jeff Barker, Tommy Youlden, John Murray, Ray Hiron, Robin Friday, Eamon Dunphy and Gary Peters who all played in the 4–1 defeat. Hurley said, 'All these players have got to fight if they're going to be in the first team to play Torquay on Saturday.'

Reading Evening Post, 20 February 1976
Charlie Hurley has given a vote of confidence to the Reading team despite three consecutive away defeats. Hurley has named the same side which finished last Friday's 4–1 defeat . . .

Reading Evening Post, 23 February 1976
Reading 0 Torquay 0

Reading Evening Post, 26 February 1976
Reading 1 Hartlepool 0
. . . Magic man Robin Friday survived a brutal kicking last night to score a goal which ended a month of miserable results . . . It's a goal which hopefully will help the club turn the corner towards the final push to promotion – and a goal which represented a fine spit in the eye to Hartlepool's tactics. Reading were just 12 minutes away from what would have been another disastrous goalless draw when Friday collected a short pass from Stewart Henderson and slotted a shot perfectly through the gap from 15 yards out. It was an ideal knock-out punch against the side whose continual fouling, spoiling and

time-wasting tactics had the fans and players beside themselves with frustration ... One is increasingly under the impression that if Friday was out for some time through injury the Reading team would fall to pieces. Fortunately, he is tough enough to survive any amount of stick *and* get precious goals like last night's which pushed the club into third place ...

ROGER TITFORD: He had a very good long shot because he could curve the ball rather than whack it. He was quite good in the air and he wouldn't give up easily. He'd chase everything and he rattled people. That made a difference.

Reading Evening Post, 1 March 1976
Huddersfield 3 Reading 0
... Reading were completely outplayed in all departments from start to finish ... To be brutally frank, Huddersfield played like a promotion side and Reading didn't ... Robin Friday was not able to produce much of his usual brilliance. He showed his frustration by getting booked in the second half for something he said after a free-kick decision, his sixth caution of the season ...

   ... Graham Taylor escaped death hours before being named Fourth Division Manager of the Month again. Taylor was driving back from a game when his car left the road in high winds on the A303 ...

ROD LEWINGTON: He came across as rebellious but not in a nasty sort of way. I never heard him use words like 'snob'. This club we went to in Sindlesham Mill was a snobbish place. Everyone who went there had money and was well dressed. Robin didn't go there to pick fights with people because they had money, he just kept out of their way. He didn't make any comment about them or sound like he was jealous of what they had.

LIZA FRIDAY: He was always at Kensington Market. Always stealing up there. Every time he went there he would buy a shirt and steal a shirt. It wasn't worth us going if he didn't steal.

Reading Evening Post, 3 March 1976

Reading 1 Newport County 0

. . . The Football League's 1–0 win specialists got away with it again last night . . .

Reading Evening Post, 8 March 1976

Reading 0, Doncaster 1

. . . This match ended Reading's sequence of 26 Fourth Division home games without defeat . . . Where previously the ball had been played accurately to the brilliant Robin Friday and he had used it to torment Doncaster defence, now he was required to chase long hopeful balls blasted in the general direction of the visitors' goal . . .

Reading Evening Post, 15 March 1976

Bradford City 1 Reading 1

Despite the heartbreak of conceding an equaliser five minutes from the end of game, Reading should have won . . .

Reading Evening Post, 18 March 1976

Reading 0 Barnsley 0

Reading slumped out of the Fourth Division's top four last night in a style which suggested they might never get back into it . . . Hollis went closest in the first half with a powerful and well-placed header when Robin Friday brilliantly got in behind the defence and crossed perfectly to him.

Reading Evening Post, 22 March 1976

Reading 4 Darlington 1

. . . Reading's rediscovery of their attacking play could not have come at a better time ... A good run by Ray Hiron, a storming burst and accurate cross by Hollis and Friday right on the spot to finish it off with his 17th goal of the season. He was booked for the seventh time this season for tripping Darlington's David Craig. Friday intends to appeal against the booking because of the persistent provocation he suffered ... Friday got some measure of justice three minutes from time when Craig was sent off for yet another foul on him ... The only surprise was that referee Donald Biddle had not taken such drastic action against Craig or Bobby Noble before ... Noble was also booked for hacking down Friday and then, in another amazing incident, Sinclair too had his name taken for bowling over Murray who had sat down on the ball, possibly to humiliate Darlington or possibly for a rest.

Reading Evening Post, 23 March 1976
Reading Football Club received a firm warning from the Football Association about their disciplinary record ... One man in particular at Elm Park who must improve his record is leading scorer Robin Friday. The club learned this week that his caution against Darlington last Saturday is worth another four points, so he now stands on 36 for the season, possibly one booking away from another three-match ban ... Maurice Evans warned today, 'Robin has got to keep his head for our last nine games. We can't afford to lose him during these few games of the season – or at the start of next season for that matter.' Friday has clearly got to mend his ways immediately for he will almost certainly be marked in tonight's crucial Fourth Division match at Stockport by a player with a comparatively bad record, Richard Dixey.

Reading Evening Post, 27 March 1976
Stockport County 1 Reading 1
Two controversially disallowed goals and a terrible goalkeeping error cost Reading a precious promotion point last night ... Reading players were still bitterly contesting the two refereeing decisions

which cost Robin Friday a memorable hat-trick . . . Only four minutes earlier Reading had every reason to be optimistic when Friday put them one up with his 18th goal of the season.

Division Four, 27 March 1976
1. Lincoln
2. Northampton
3. Tranmere
4. Reading

Reading Evening Post, 1 April 1976
Reading 5 Tranmere Rovers 0
Top referee Clive Thomas takes charge of matches all over the world – European Cup, World Cup, he's seen the best football. For Clive Thomas last night it was not a big occasion, Reading versus Tranmere in the Fourth Division – just another match. Thomas has a big reputation for ice-cold temperament. He was unemotional, undemonstrative, but last night Thomas saw something he couldn't believe in the feet of Robin Friday, the 23-year-old Reading striker who just two seasons ago was playing in the lowly Isthmian League. In one brilliant move Friday tugged down a loose ball, sprung around, slotted the ball into the top corner of the net: 10,961 fans were still and Thomas clapped. He held his head in his hands in frank disbelief. I can't believe a player like that isn't in the First Division, it was an amazing goal . . . so stunning in its execution that it will surely be talked about as long as football is played at Elm Park.

CLIVE THOMAS, REFEREE: I'll never forget it. It was the sheer ferocity of the shot on the volley from the halfway line over his shoulder. I just could not believe it at the time. If it hadn't gone into the top corner of the net it would have broken the goalpost. Even up against the likes of Pele and Cruyff, it still rates as the best goal I have ever seen.

ALF FRIDAY: At the time I didn't realise it was such a good goal.

DAVID DOWNS, READING FC HISTORIAN: The ball is played up to him from midfield and he has his back to goal. He controls it with his chest, sets it up, the ball just pops up for him and he volleys it over his shoulder without even turning. He turned after the ball was gone.

SYD SIMMONDS: Robin had his back to goal right on the edge of the box. He took the ball on his chest, dropped it off his chest and as the ball came down he turned and hit it. The ball just flew in. It was brilliant. I'd never seen anything like it.

CLIVE THOMAS, REFEREE: After the game I went up to him and said, 'I have to tell you that that is the best goal I have ever seen.' Robin just looked at me and said, 'Really? You should come down here more often. I do that every week.'

TONY FRIDAY: When we were kids we were in a very good side in the Fulham League, premier division. One particular day, and I'll always remember this, I had the ball out wide, came back on myself and chipped it over the centre-half's head. Robin volleyed it in full stride. I didn't see that goal against Tranmere. I was in the warehouse [prison] for a lot of the time he was at Reading. But I would imagine it was similar – and, on a Sunday morning, to see a goal like that, was brilliant.

Reading Evening Post, 2 April 1976
Staking his reputation on Reading's footballing success, a Walgrave man decided the team could do with beefing up. Mr Peter Jennings decided to offer an additional pound bonus per month if the team defeated Tranmere on Wednesday night – a pound of best rump steaks. After the 5–0 thrashing of Tranmere he came around to Elm

Park to hand over the meat. Mr Jennings, of L.J. Jennings Butchers, High Street, offered the steaks – 12 one-pounders – to the manager before the game but the news was kept secret from the team.

Reading Evening Post, 3 April 1976
Rochdale 0 Reading 0

Reading Evening Post, 5 April 1976
Reading star striker Robin Friday should be fit enough to play in the important Fourth Division match at Bournemouth on Wednesday. His badly bruised shin should not prevent him from turning out at Dene Court. His fitness will be a big boost to his team-mates, who obviously missed his inspiration when the game was affected by injury at the goalless draw on Saturday. Friday was struggling from the very first minute when he was victim of an over-the-ball foul. With so much at stake for the club and so much depending on Friday himself, it is a pity he can't be persuaded to wear shinpads. Even with Friday limping, however, the point Reading collected was enough to take them back into third place.

Reading Evening Post, 8 April 1976
Bournemouth 0 Reading 1
Friday, playing his 100th league game, had another brilliant one . . . He headed across the goal to the unmarked Nelson . . . who took it down on the chest and ferociously lashed it into the top corner from the edge of the six-yard box.

Reading Evening Post, 10 April 1976
Elm Park this afternoon will stage what should be one of its most memorable games in the last ten years, when Reading take on Fourth Division leaders Lincoln City . . .

Reading Evening Post, 12 April 1976
Reading 1 Lincoln City 1

Graham Taylor, manager of already-promoted Lincoln City, said, 'Reading will have to go some to miss out on promotion now. I am confident we will be playing with them in Division Three next season.' Reading need a maximum of five points from four games to be certain of going up.

Reading Evening Post, 13 April 1976
. . . Beware of the amazing hallucinatory mushrooms. While they are legal, they do odd things to the soup. An expert warned that the danger lurks in our woods and grasslands when a couple who picked dozens of liberty cap mushrooms at Heckfield were cleared of possession. The small white mushroom contains a drug which has similar effects to LSD.

Reading Evening Post, 15 April 1976
Northampton 4 Reading 1
Reading look back in anger . . . Not only should they not have been heavily beaten at County, they should have had the game comfortably sewn up by half-time. If you didn't see the game you will find it hard to believe in view of the scoreline. If you did see the game you will find the scoreline almost impossible to believe.

MAURICE EVANS: I remember going round to pick Robin up for this away game and Liza was shouting and bawling at him, following him all the way down the road. He got on the coach with the lads and she was still stood outside shouting and swearing at him. But that was normal.

SHEILA FRIDAY: Charlie didn't want Robin to marry Liza, did he?

CHARLIE HURLEY: One day this woman phoned up and said, 'I want to come and see you with my daughter.' I said, 'What's it about?' She said, 'It's to do with Robin Friday.' I thought, 'We've got a problem.' So she brings this girl over and all kinds of things are going through my mind. I gave her a cup of tea, sat her down and said, 'What do you want?' She replied, 'My daughter is going to marry Robin Friday.' I said, 'Are you pregnant?' She replied, 'No.' I said, 'You can't do that then.' The mother said, 'Why?' I said, 'Because he's mad. You can't marry him. He's a footballer not a husband at all. It's hard enough for him to be a footballer. He can't be a husband.' The mother said, 'Well, it doesn't matter because my daughter is mad as well.' There was no answer to that.

Reading Evening Post, 19 April 1976
After half a century without success Reading Football Club hope to mark the Queen's 50th birthday with celebrations of their own. It was back in 1926, the same year the Queen was born, that Reading last tasted promotion. Now the two events come together again on the very same day. Go to it, Reading.

Reading Evening Post, 20 April 1976
Reading 1 Brentford 0
Just one point from promotion. Abracadabra and Friday's magic puts Reading on the brink . . . A moment of magic from battered Robin Friday yesterday put Reading just one point away from promotion. Limping badly after an unmerciful kicking, he beat three men and crashed the ball against the post. It was left for Ray Hiron to ram home for his third goal in three games . . . Reading can clinch it tomorrow. Now for Cambridge and Friday's fit . . .

Reading Evening Post, 22 April 1976
Cambridge 2 Reading 2
Hurley's Heroes . . . Reading arrived in the Third Division last night on a flood of champagne . . . They drew 2–2 at Cambridge to clinch promotion. Reading skipper Gordon Cumming led his players from

their champagne celebrations to greet the fans. The players threw their blue-and-white shirts to the fans from the pitch but the supporters still would not leave, calling for the man who guided the club up, Charlie Hurley. Hurley finally appeared from the dressing-room half an hour after the final whistle to tell them, 'You're the people we do it for' . . . Celebrations started at a premature stage as Ray Hiron got a near-post flick on Eamon Dunphy's right-wing corner for Robin Friday to come storming in at the far post and smash home with his left foot for his 21st goal of the season . . .

Charlie Hurley promised Reading supporters a champagne farewell to Fourth Division football, 'We're hoping for 20,000 at Elm Park and we are planning to give them a hell of a send-off.'

CHARLIE HURLEY: When our lads won promotion we went to Cambridge and we were two-nil up. Robin was a real talent that day because he was desperate to win promotion. Then we kicked up the hill in the second half and we got to two-each. Then Cambridge nearly got the winner through bad defending on our side. I was sitting in the dugout and I jumped up and knocked a great big board out of the top of this dugout and I didn't even know that I had done it. The pressure is tremendous. I won very little as regards trophies as a player. In fact, I don't think I won any. I got promotion with Sunderland – but we didn't get a trophy because we were runners-up. Won promotion at Reading – didn't get a trophy. I got a lot of caps, I was voted Ireland's Footballer of the Year, I've been made Sunderland's Player of the Century and I won the first Hall of Fame for Ireland's Greatest International. But I won these things as an individual and I always wanted to win things as a team. That was my ambition.

DAVID DOWNS: After the game at Cambridge they stopped off at a hotel for a celebration dinner and drink. In this hotel Gordon Cummings saw some nice fluted wine glasses on the table, saying, 'I wouldn't mind a few of them for home.' Robin said, 'Give us a few minutes and I'll get them for you.' So he went round the dining-room and ended up with a full box of these glasses, which he took out of the hotel. When they got back on the coach Robin decided he didn't want to give the glasses to Gordon. Cummings thought this was wrong. It was all right to steal from the hotel but it was wrong not to give them to him.

Reading Evening Post, 24 April 1976
. . . Celebration day at Elm Park today when Reading take on Crewe in what will hopefully be their last ever Fourth Division game. The season, which started like many others with so much hope, has ended with triumph. This afternoon the players want to say thank you to the fans who have supported them throughout the season.

Reading Evening Post, 26 April 1976
Reading 3 Crewe Alexandra 1
. . . Robin Friday and Gordon Cumming are still arguing about which one of them scored the goal. Yesterday's Southern Television failed to prove whether Cumming had pushed the ball in before crossing the line from Friday's foot. Said Cumming: 'Even after watching the film I got a touch. If Robin wants to claim it, good luck to him. What's one goal between friends when you've won promotion.' Friday said, 'I am claiming the goal. It was definitely mine.' The club officially credited it to him and took his season's tally to 22.
. . . QPR were this morning denying that there had been yet another flare-up between Dave Sexton and Stan Bowles. Bowles refused to fly to Israel with the rest of the team for a five-day tour and is reported to have exchanged angry words with Sexton at the airport . . .

Reading Evening Post, 29 April 1976
Reading's leading scorer Robin Friday plans to make a plea to the FA

Disciplinary Committee next week to be allowed to play at the start of the club's Third Division campaign in August. Friday learnt today that he received four points for his booking against Cambridge when Reading gained promotion. It takes his total for the season to over 40 points and he must serve another ban. Normally the suspension would be for three matches but Reading's 22-goal player of the year will plead for leniency.

Reading Evening Post, 30 April 1976
The England star Kevin Keegan was voted Footballer of the Year last night by the Football Association.

Reading Evening Post, 7 May 1976
Reading star striker Robin Friday was today thanking his lucky stars that he has been banned from just one game at the start of next season. This week's decision by the FA Disciplinary Committee means that Friday will not miss any games at the start of the club's new Third Division campaign. Instead, he will be suspended from Reading's Football League Cup first-round first-leg game on 14 August. Friday, with 22 goals . . . also totalled 40 points over the season for eight bookings and one sending-off . . . Charlie Hurley said, 'Robin is as pleased as punch because this is the first time that anyone in authority has tried to be fair with him. Now there is a genuine opportunity for him to mend his ways and he is really going to take it next season.' The FA also studied the report of his last booking at Cambridge when Brendan Batson was sent off for kicking him . . .

. . . Fiona Richmond today defended her nude bath with Crystal Palace footballers and said she didn't think it contributed to last night's departure of club manager Malcolm Allison . . .

CHARLIE HURLEY: If his attitude away from the pitch was as good as it was on the pitch, we wouldn't have held on to him. He would have gone for £100,000, because when we got promotion lots of clubs phoned up and asked about him.

SYD SIMMONDS: When Reading got promotion Robin got a big bonus. Liza had moved into the flat with us. He booked this holiday to Gibraltar for them. He said to me, 'You come as well.' 'Nah,' I said, 'I'll be all right.' On the Saturday morning, the day they were flying, he got Liza's suitcase, emptied it and said, 'Put your clothes in there, we're off.' Fuck it, off we went. Liza and Carol, my girlfriend, caught up with us at the airport. They were shouting and screaming at us but we had just got through Customs. Robin shouted, 'We'll send you a ticket tomorrow.' We never did.

ROD LEWINGTON: He liked his own space. When you could get him on his own you realised that. That was when he was very sort of quiet and he talked sensibly. When he was out, had a few drinks, a couple of smokes, he didn't know when to stop. That was the thing. As long as there was something going on he wanted to be there. On the other hand, I think he was looking for something but didn't know what it was. You could sense that when you were talking to him on his own. Sometimes you got the impression he didn't want all the hype. I think he thought he had been put on a pedestal and had to live up to what he was portrayed to be, although he wasn't necessarily like that.

EAMON DUNPHY: When we won promotion we got screwed by the club. We didn't get what we had been promised. They acted very badly. At that stage the whole team lost faith in the board and in Hurley and in the club. There was a butcher who supported us and he gave the club a load of meat and we got the mince steak while the board kept the fillet steaks for themselves – which didn't go down very well. I think that summer we all realised what arseholes they were. Robin as well. At that stage morale plummeted. For Robin, that was his excuse to go back to living wild. It was a big disappointment for him, a big disappointment for all of us.

Album release, 22 May 1976: *Rastaman Vibration* by Bob Marley and the Wailers.

Reading Evening Post, 4 June 1976
Reading Football Club kick off next season in Division Three with an away match against Gillingham on 21 August.

Robin Friday has asked for a transfer. His request is sure to be discussed at Reading's next board meeting. It is likely he will be told he must stay . . . Friday, 23, handed a transfer request to the club's chairman Frank Waller immediately after he'd met all the players to discuss the new contracts. 'I want to find a club who will pay me the sort of wage I think I am worth and a club with a little bit of ambition, preferably one in the London area. I have worked my guts out to help get Reading out of the Fourth Division and this offer seems to be all the thanks I get. Quite simply I want a bigger basic wage than the one that Reading are offering me and I am concerned that there doesn't seem to be any ambition in Elm Park. If you ask me, they would be happy to stroll along in the bottom half of the Third Division for ever. I don't think I am being big-headed if I say that I put quite a few on the gates at Elm Park. Now I would rather play in the higher division. I did all right in the Fourth Division and I've confidence in my abilities to do better.' The long-haired striker was also voted Reading's Player of the Year for the second consecutive season. During the season manager Charlie Hurley turned down a £60,000 bid for him from Cardiff City. But Friday insists, 'I'm determined to get away from Elm Park. If necessary I will take my case to the Football League tribunal like Dick Habbin did a couple of years ago.' Friday is getting married for the second time at St James's Church, Reading, next week.

Reading Evening Post, 5 August 1976
The Elm Park dressing-room pay row is almost over. Nearly all the Reading players, including Robin Friday, have signed or will shortly be signing new contracts with the club. While Friday settled his differences with Reading, another player, John Murray, has requested a move.

LIZA FRIDAY: His mother gave me a small silver football boot and insisted I wore it, which I did, around my waist.

ROD LEWINGTON: At his wedding he invited everybody he could possibly think of. There must have been two hundred people there. It was on a Sunday and Robin turned up in a brown velvet suit, a tigerskin sort of shirt, open at the neck, and snakeskin boots. Southern TV cameras were there and Robin sat on the steps of the church and rolled a joint in front of them. Everyone was smoking. The bride showed up. We went into the church and the whole congregation was laughing because of the smoke. The vicar was laughing because he thought, 'What a happy congregation.' But they were all out of their brains. Then we went to the reception in Watlington Street, the grounds of a big old house there. And Robin was rolling these joints and handing them out to the relations, all these elderly aunties and uncles. By half past one that afternoon there wasn't a sober person there. They were either pissed or completely out of it. All these old women had their skirts stuffed into their knickers and were jumping around the lawn and I just don't know what the vicar thought. I have been to a few weddings but never one like that.

Reading Evening Post, 8 August 1976
It's been quite a week of contract-signing for Reading soccer star Robin Friday. After signing a new contract with the Elm Park club, Robin entered into a quite different one with Liza Deimel on Saturday. Robin and Liza, both 24, were married in church as his

colleagues beat Charlton in a pre-season friendly. Liza was given away by her father, Mr Whithold Deimel, wearing a full-length cream dress with a small silver football boot hanging from her waist. She carried orchids. The Reading venue was kept secret but the road outside the church was still packed with people. Robin will shortly be starting his third season with Reading. The couple had a short honeymoon in Amsterdam and Robin was back at Elm Park today to continue training. The couple will be setting up home in Tilehurst Road.

LIZA FRIDAY: The wedding was the most hilarious thing ever. They came in their droves from London, they nicked all their wedding presents, they started beating each other up. Everyone was sitting round smoking dope, anything that had wedding paper on it went. By the time the whole thing was over we'd been stripped. My mother was going, 'I don't believe this.' We went to Amsterdam for our honeymoon and someone had given Robin a big lump of dope for a wedding present. I think loads of people did, because I was saying, 'These people haven't given us a present,' and he had pockets full of dope. When we got to Amsterdam airport he was speeding and he was paranoid. So he put all the dope in his mouth because he thought we were going to be searched – but he was also chewing gum. We spent the night – my wedding night – trying to separate the dope from the chewing gum and the more he tried to separate it the more it got on his fingers and the more aggravated he got. Some honeymoon. The next day we went on one of those canal boats and he was off looking for drugs within five minutes.

Reading Evening Post, 13 August 1976
George Best, the former Ireland and Manchester United footballer, today vowed he will marry and settle down when he returns to England this year to play . . .

LIZA FRIDAY: In 1976, when the summer was really glorious, we went down to St Ives in Cornwall and for me it was a really special time – not that other times weren't special but it was just him and me. The weather was great, he was drug-free, apart from a bit of dope, and it was fantastic.

CHARLIE HURLEY: He lost his way when we got promotion. He really must have celebrated all through the summer. He was in the headlines – 'Friday is the King' – and it went to his head. When he came back he was very unfit and his asthma was giving him a hard time. He was trying his hardest but he had lost a yard of pace. So I had him in the office and said, 'What have you been doing in the summer? You finished the season bright as a button – easily the most exciting player in the Fourth Division never mind the Third which we're into now. You've got to remember it's slightly different class in the Third – these guys are going to wind you up.' He said, 'I've got a few problems, boss.' I said, 'Since when haven't you had loads of problems, kid?' He said, 'I know but I'm married now.'

Reading Evening Post, 16 August 1976
Reading 2 Peterborough Utd 3, League Cup first round (first leg)
. . . Reading will have to raise their game a lot more if they are going to survive in the Third . . .

Reading Evening Post, 17 August 1976
Peterborough 0 Reading 1, League Cup first round (second leg)
For the second time in a few days Reading have raised our hopes of a successful Third Division campaign by playing one of the best teams in this section. And last night they not only outplayed Peterborough but they beat them on their own ground, to force a third meeting to decide this League Cup first-round thriller . . . Friday was eight yards out with all the time and space he wanted. It

was a simple chance, not the sort Friday misses, but he still managed to do something out of the ordinary, threading his shot through the goalkeeper's legs . . . Sadly Friday's evening was again marred by a booking, this time for a tackle from behind on Greg Lee after 25 minutes. So his record this season is now two goals and two cautions in two games and, while it is impossible to have any sympathy for Friday's disciplinary misdemeanours, it must be said that far, far worse fouls, including two particularly nasty ones from Friday himself, went unpunished last night. Friday's goal certainly roused Peterborough but Reading had learned the lesson of last Saturday and were in no mood to capitulate in the last ten minutes as they did in the first match.

Reading Evening Post, 23 August 1976
Gillingham 2 Reading 2
The Elm Park club drew 2–2 after leading 2–0 . . . A last-gasp equaliser for Gillingham . . .

Reading Evening Post, 27 August 1976
Peterborough 3 Reading 1, League Cup first round (replay)
At 1–1 the game went into extra-time . . . In the extra half-hour Reading were effectively a man short as Robin Friday was so badly crippled by the kicking he received . . . If they'd won they'd have had the pleasure of taking on Fulham where George Best plays in a money-spinning second-round tie at Craven Cottage . . .

Reading Evening Post, 27 August 1976
. . . Robin Friday boosted Reading's chances of a good result at Shrewsbury by passing a fitness test at Elm Park this morning. He kept his place in the side which showed two changes from the team beaten 3–1 in the League Cup replay on Wednesday.

Reading Evening Post, 30 August 1976
Shrewsbury 2 Reading 0

. . . Despite the usual impressive performance by Friday, Reading's 2–0 defeat against Shrewsbury on Saturday was almost entirely due to their failure to take their scoring chances.

. . . Reading may now be preparing to sell their star player to a First Division club. I understand Reading have received a bid for Friday and are considering whether to let him go. It could be that they take the view that by selling Friday they will gain enough money to buy two or three other players to strengthen their Third Division side . . . .

. . . George Best revealed today that he is to be married again in Berkshire within a few weeks. He will start a fresh career in British football after six months in the United States.

Reading Evening Post, 4 September 1976
Third Division soccer makes its long-awaited return to Elm Park this afternoon.

Reading Evening Post, 6 September 1976
Reading 2 Walsall 1
. . . The first goal came after only three minutes and was a penalty kick . . . The second, nine minutes from time, was a result of Robin Friday's one moment of magic . . . Walsall's Eire international goalkeeper Mick Kerns was to blame for leaving the box and challenging first Dennis Nelson and then Friday with his feet . . . Friday won the ball easily from him but still had no easy task with two defenders blocking goal . . . However, from 35 yards out Friday's chip was so perfect that Colin Harrison had no option but to use his hands to keep it out the top corner . . . Friday had a disappointing game but for this one moment of exquisite skill.

Reading Evening Post, 7 September 1976
Reading 2 Wrexham 0
. . . For the second time in five days Reading beat a very, very good side at Elm Park. Under the cosh for most of the game, they showed

tremendous spirit . . . There seemed no danger when Tommy Youlden finally struck a long ball down the middle into the crowded penalty area. The ball rebounded off Murray straight into the path of Robin Friday who volleyed it first time into the left-hand corner from 18 yards . . .

Division One, 7 September 1976
1. Liverpool
2. Middlesbrough
3. Manchester City

Division Two, 7 September 1976
1. Blackpool
2. Bolton
3. Oldham

Division Three, 7 September 1976
1. Mansfield
2. Swindon
3. Rotherham

Division Four, 7 September 1976
1. Stockport
2. Bournemouth
3. Bradford

Reading Evening Post, 13 September 1976
Northampton Town 1 Reading 2
. . . Reading's third win on the trot . . .

Reading Evening Post, 14 September 1976
Friday out as Reading go for top . . . Reading will be without star striker Robin Friday for tonight's match. Friday is in bed with flu and his place goes to Mick Hollis. The loss of Friday, top scorer and

player of the year for the last two seasons, is a huge blow to Reading.

Reading Evening Post, 16 September 1976
Peterborough Town 2 Reading 1

Thursday Night TV, 16 September 1976
BBC1: *Tomorrow's World, Top of the Pops, Happy Ever After, Kojak, Sailor, Gangsters*
ITV: *Crossroads, Bionic Woman, Frankie Howerd, Shaft, What the Papers Say, Roger Snow reads extracts from the Bible*

Reading Evening Post, 17 September 1976
Robin Friday is named as Reading's sub for tomorrow. The popular striker has missed most of the week's training after going down with flu but he reported back to Elm Park yesterday. Friday hasn't done any serious training and Charlie Hurley thought it would be too much of a gamble to play him.

Reading Evening Post, 23 September 1976
. . . Robin Friday, who played at Ninian Park after missing two first-team games, is set for a recall. The reserves went two goals ahead but Cardiff responded and got two in the second half.

Joe Frasier is due to join Ken Norton's training camp to give his old sparring-partner tips on how to beat world heavyweight champion Muhammad Ali . . .

Reading Evening Post, 26 September 1976
Portsmouth 2 Reading 2

Reading Evening Post, 28 September 1976
. . . Muhammad Ali said he was considering retiring following a unanimous but unpopular 15-man decision over Ken Norton . . .

Reading Evening Post, 2 October 1976
. . . George Best was sent off for dissent in the second half of the game with Southampton versus Fulham.

Reading Evening Post, 4 October 1976
Reading 4 Swindon 1
Magnificent Reading turned in a brilliant performance to hammer Swindon in the local derby . . .

Reading Evening Post, 11 October 1976
Chesterfield 4 Reading 0
. . . A ninth-minute goal put Reading on the way to their third defeat of the season at Chesterfield this afternoon . . .

CHARLIE HURLEY: He was playing against these Third Division sides that he could normally have turned inside out – and suddenly he had lost a yard and his control of the ball was not as good. Tommy Youlden said to me, 'What's up with Robin?' I told him it was something that you and I will never know.

MAURICE EVANS: I kept saying to Charlie, 'You're going to have to get rid of him.' See, the players found it hard to accept Robin's ways. The crowd didn't – they love someone like that. But the players? When Robin didn't come in for three days they all wanted to know, 'What's happening with Robin? We're working every day and he comes in for two days a week. There is something wrong here.' Charlie would fob them off with some excuse, but that's what happened. It was chaos and therefore discipline was difficult to uphold. The players kept pointing at Robin and saying, 'What are you going to do about him?' From the outside it looked as if Charlie wasn't doing anything. He most certainly did try to master Robin but, as I say, it was very, very hard.

DAVID DOWNS: Quite a few big clubs, so the story went, came down to see him. I think QPR were interested for a while, and West Ham, but I think what put them off was his temperament. They weren't sure that they could handle him.

LIZA FRIDAY: He left Reading because Charlie Hurley, who liked Robin and had a lot of time for Robin, knew he was using drugs. He used to come to the flat endlessly and say, 'The squad needs you but I owe it to the club because I can't have you using drugs.' Lots of big clubs were coming in for Robin and Charlie would say to him, 'You have got to be fair to me. If *I* know you're using drugs it won't take *them* long to find out. You have got to get your act together. Or I'll have to give you a free transfer.' Charlie really liked Robin, and for Robin's own sake he wanted him to stop.

Reading Evening Post, 16 October 1976
Reading 0 Sheffield Wednesday 1
Reading went down to a thoroughly professional display by Sheffield Wednesday today . . . Fighting broke out between groups of supporters ten minutes before the start.

Reading Evening Post, 19 October 1976
Reading boss Charlie Hurley is one of the favourites for the vacant manager's job at Sunderland. Hurley, 12 years a Sunderland player, is known to be interested in the position . . .

Reading Evening Post, 25 October 1976
Lincoln City 3 Reading 1
Reading crashed at Lincoln after a burst of three goals in four minutes at the start of the second half.

MAURICE EVANS: Charlie said to me, 'We're going to have to get rid of him.' Robin was running the club. He'd taken charge.

Everyone loved him and he could do what he wanted. So he was going to have to go.

Reading Evening Post, 28 October 1976
Reading Football Club today announced they have put star striker Robin Friday on the transfer list at his own request . . . they imagine that Friday will certainly not be sold for less than £50,000 . . . Hurley said today, 'Robin's ambition is to play in a higher division than the Third or Fourth and the Board and I don't want to stand in his way.' . . . If they do sell Friday it could be in a player-plus-cash deal so Reading will have the cash available for the wholesale rebuilding they require . . . The decision to let Friday go is sure to be controversial with the fans . . . Apart from being Reading's most exciting player, he has been their top scorer and Player of the Year for the last two seasons. But he evidently feels his game would benefit from a change of club . . . Friday has attracted plenty of First Division scouts during the past year but so far only Cardiff City, who were then in the Third Division, made a definite bid. Their £60,000 offer last year was firmly rejected. Another Division Three club, Crystal Palace, made an enquiry about him earlier this month and could well still be interested.

Reading Evening Post, 1 November 1976
Reading 2 Chester 0
. . . Ray Hiron's biggest contribution was to take the pressure off Robin Friday who was consequently able to end his long spell without a goal, a priceless early goal which gave Reading the initiative . . . Transfer-seeking Friday was then able to get in more goalscoring positions and he could have finished with a hat-trick . . .

Reading Evening Post, 2 November 1976
. . . England manager Don Revie today ended the arguments which have raged over Stan Bowles by calling on the controversial Queen's

Park Rangers striker to join his squad for the World Cup qualifying match against Italy in Rome.

Reading Evening Post, 4 November 1976
Reading 2 Brighton 3

. . . Reading were still trying to work out today how they managed to outplay the top team in the Third Division, create a dozen good scoring chances and still lose . . . Of course the reason they lost is the simplest in the game: they failed to put away enough of those easy chances . . .

Reading Evening Post, 8 November 1976
Crystal Palace 1 Reading 1

. . . Crystal Palace didn't have anyone up front with the skill of Robin Friday, whose goal and all-round performance could well have persuaded the London club to renew their interest in him . . . Friday's 37th-minute goal, which came so close to winning the game for Reading, was a beauty . . . Friday got up before the keeper and passed him with an Alan Gilzean-type flick . . .

Reading Evening Post, 9 November 1976
Mansfield Town 4 Reading 0

. . . Reading turned in a stinker last night . . . Charlie Hurley brought on Bruce Stuckey to replace Robin Friday, who had been marked out of the game by Mansfield's Colin Foster . . . Coincidence or not, when Friday left so did half a dozen managers and scouts . . .

DAVID DOWNS: Apparently he was taken off injured against Mansfield and crapped in their bath. He was that kind of outlandish character.

Reading Evening Post, 15 November 1976
Reading 0 Preston North End 2

. . . The most appalling display at Elm Park for years . . .

Reading Evening Post, 27 November 1976
Tranmere Rovers 2 Reading 1

Reading Evening Post, 30 November 1976
. . . Charlie Hurley said, 'I keep picking up the Sunday papers which say that people are interested in Friday, but since I put him on the transfer list not one club has come in for him . . .'

Reading Evening Post, 2 December 1976
Bill Grundy, television interviewer, has spoken about the interview which shocked viewers last night with the foul language of rock group The Sex Pistols . . .

Reading Evening Post, 4 December 1976
Frost KO's vital Elm Park match . . .

Reading Evening Post, 11 December 1976
Reading's game against Wycombe has been postponed . . .

Reading Evening Post, 14 December 1976
Wycombe Wanderers 1 Reading 2, FA Cup second round
Reading reached the third round of the FA Cup at Wycombe this afternoon after a spirited struggle by the non-league side. Reading's task on a hard, frost-bound ground was never easy, even after Robin Friday had shot them into a fifth-minute lead and then added a second half an hour later. There was fighting on the terraces before the kick-off and the police had to take four youths out of the ground . . .

Reading Evening Post, 15 December 1976
Charlie Hurley's FA Cup luck ran out when they were drawn against Second Division Hereford United in the third round, just about the worse possible draw they could have received. As Hurley said, 'It's a stinker, an absolute shocker.'

Reading Evening Post, 20 December 1976
Grimsby Town 2 Reading 1
It looks like being an unhappy Christmas for Reading Football Club
– and they could face a long battle against relegation in the New
Year . . .

LIZA FRIDAY: From my point of view he was definitely not the
man to marry because he received real adulation from female
fans. I used to go and meet the team coach after away matches
and he would always have got off early. He'd say to his team-
mates, 'I don't care what you tell the wife.' Ten men would get
off the bus and I'd be standing there going, 'The bastard has got
away again' and he'd be off to some club or other.

CHARLIE HURLEY: If he hadn't got married I think he would have
been all right. I'm not on about Liza – I'm talking about him
personally. He could not accept responsibility. The best part of
his career, if you look, was when he was single.

ROD LEWINGTON: Robin should probably never have got married.
But don't forget he was a young guy – he had more than he had
had before and there was no one in town who hadn't heard of
him.

Reading Evening Post, 23 December 1976
. . . Four games in the space of eight days presents a wonderful
opportunity for Reading to improve their lowly Division Three
position.

MAURICE EVANS: Just before Christmas we went to an away game
and Jimmy Andrews, the Cardiff City manager, was there just to
give the deal the final nod. Robin played ever so well. The
players' bar was right next to the directors' room and Charlie

Hurley took me aside and said, 'Go in there and make sure Robin is okay' – because he would go in there and drink about six pints in ten minutes and be all over the place. Sure enough, I go in there and Robin has drunk three pints already. Jimmy Andrews was just coming in and I'm trying to shield him because Robin is half gone.

CHARLIE HURLEY: When Jimmy Andrews came in with the 30 grand I went to the directors and they were happy with it because they knew Robin had lost his way a bit. There was an awful lot more to it than that, but we accepted the 30 grand. I took a tremendous amount of stick for the deal but I'd never tell people the real reason because I would never ever run down Robin Friday. I'd rather take all the flak and let them think I was the silly prat who sold him for 30 grand.

LIZA FRIDAY: Robin was never happy about moving to Cardiff: too far, Second Division and he wanted more. But Charlie Hurley had said, 'If you don't quit I'm getting rid of you quickly. I can't send you to a big club while this is going on.' There was a lot of conflict about the money that should have gone to Reading because Jimmy Andrews knew something was amiss which is why Reading let Robin go for such a small amount.

MAURICE EVANS: In the end Jimmy Andrews took him despite all his worries.

Reading Evening Post, 28 December 1976
Reading I Peterborough Utd 0
Reading ease relegation with a I–0 win over Peterborough . . .
John Murray scored the only goal from a free-kick in the 17th minute.

Reading Evening Post, 30 December 1976
Robin Friday was set to sign for Cardiff City today. Cardiff manager
Jimmy Andrews announced that his club have agreed terms with
Reading at £30,000. Transfer-listed Friday was travelling to Wales to
talk terms. Andrews hopes to sign him in time to make his début in
Saturday's home game against Fulham. Charlie Hurley confirmed
that the club had been enquiring about Robin but that nothing
definite has been decided . . . This season Friday's form has not been
so impressive and he has only scored seven goals so far. At the same
time he has constantly been trying to find a club in a higher division
and now it looks as if he's got his wish.

Reading Evening Post, 30 December 1976
Oxford 1 Reading 0
. . . To add to their misery, fans have learned that this was the last
time they'll ever see Robin Friday in a Reading shirt . . . Friday will
make his début against Fulham who expect to include George Best
as well as Bobby Moore at Ninian Park tomorrow. Friday said, 'I
wanted to get away from Reading and am delighted to have joined
Cardiff, a club with a lot of potential. I must admit the move took
me completely by surprise although I knew Cardiff were interested
last season.' . . . He now has a good chance of playing in Europe as
Cardiff are hot favourites to win the Welsh Cup and gain a place in
the European Cup-Winners' Cup.

CHARLIE HURLEY: He came up to me when he left and said, 'I
know what you're doing, boss.' I replied, 'If you know why I'm
doing it, I'm delighted. So explain to me, why d'you think I'm
doing it?' He said, 'I'm not the same player, am I?' I said, 'There
are an awful amount of things in life that are very important to
me: family, friends, football and honesty. And you've hit the nail
on the head. You are not playing half as good as you did last
season but I'm not one of those guys who's glad to be right after

the event. I really do hope that you do great at Cardiff. You've got something that is unique but you've also got a lot of problems. You're not the player you were last year and you've got married. Now, that's no bloody good, is it?'

1977: The Welsh Wilderness

JIMMY ANDREWS, CARDIFF CITY MANAGER: I saw him several times at Reading and he was absolutely outstanding. He looked all wrong, his feet pointed the wrong way, he slouched, his hair was long and unkempt – but boy could he play. I couldn't believe we got him for that price, it was an absolute steal. I knew there had to be something wrong with him, but I didn't care. I'd seen what he could do on the pitch.

JOHN MURRAY: On the coach he would drop his trousers, bare his arse, moon at people, get his privates out. He'd throw bottles out of the coach and onto the motorway. Sometimes he was funny, but other times he was completely dangerous.

RITCHIE MORGAN, CARDIFF TEAM-MATE AND CLUB CAPTAIN: I can vividly remember my first encounter with Robin Friday. It was when he was a Reading player and we were travelling back on the Cardiff coach from an away game. We were crawling through traffic in London and our coach pulled up alongside Reading's in heavy traffic. The two coaches drew level at traffic lights and both teams were giving each other plenty of good-natured stick when suddenly Robin Friday gets out of the Reading coach and into a black cab waiting alongside. He then pulls down his trousers and pants and hangs his arse out of the rear window, mooning at us. The lights change to green and the cab roars off with Robin's naked arse still hanging out of the window, bouncing all the way up the Mall. Both coaches were in absolute hysterics. Typical Robin, that was.

Jimmy Andrews didn't have to wait very long to discover the many off-field quirks of Robin's character. On the day he joined Cardiff, Robin stepped off the train from Reading clutching only a platform ticket and was promptly arrested by the British Transport Police.

HARRY PARSONS, CLUB OFFICIAL: We'd heard he could be elusive, so I just presumed he'd decided not to bother turning up. Then we got a phone call from the police telling us they had a young man in their custody who claimed to be Cardiff City's new star striker and would we care to come and collect him from the station.

PHIL DWYER, TEAM-MATE (AND CARDIFF CITY RECORD APPEARANCE HOLDER): I think a lot of the boys were shocked when Robin first turned up for training in just a T-shirt, tracksuit bottoms and a carrier-bag. He was a fearsome-looking character who used to frighten not only the opposition but his own team-mates as well. He frequently used to have to be calmed down during training – he'd be charging around like a lunatic hurtling into people. He just liked to win, that was all. But I always got on well with him. He'd have a go at me and I'd always have a go back. Before matches he'd be so hyped up, he'd never sit still in the dressing-room. He had so much skill. If someone had got hold of him and channelled his exuberance in the right direction there's no telling how far he could have gone. I never had any inclination that he was into drugs. We knew he had a reputation as a wild man before he joined us because we'd heard about him when Reading used to play Newport, so the lads all knew who Robin Friday was. Because of his reputation I think a lot of them were very surprised that the club had agreed to buy him.

RITCHIE MORGAN: He was deceptively quick over a few yards. He wasn't the quickest thing I've ever seen but once he'd got up a head of steam, he took some stopping. To a striker that first six or seven yards is so important because it can get you in front of people and Robin was like George Best in that respect, very quick off the mark to get into dangerous situations. His speed of thought was phenomenal – he'd also see things that no one else would.

PAUL WENT, EX-TEAM-MATE AND ROBIN'S ROOM-MATE: Robin and I got on from day one. We had played against each other before when he was at Reading and I was at Fulham. We'd had a battle that day, and he obviously remembered our little encounter because when I met him at Cardiff, the first thing he said was, 'Oh yeah, I remember you, you mistimed a tackle and left a scar on my fucking leg.' We had a good laugh about it. So while he had never forgiven me until he came to Cardiff, in a way he had a little bit of respect for me. He was very much an extrovert. No one could control him when his head went. But in the process of him losing it, I, probably more than anyone else, would be able to help him keep a lid on it. I loved the guy.

Out on the pitch, Robin was everybody's minder. But I used to take it upon myself to look after him. It was my job to put an arm round him and try and pacify him. Unfortunately, because I was a centre-half and he was a centre-forward, by the time I had raced up the field to get to him, the damage had usually already been done. He was the type to explode at anything but boy did he take some stick from the opposition. He could dish it out too, but he took more than any other player I've ever seen. I remember we were training once, playing five-a-side, and I was in goal. I threw the ball out and it hit him on the back of the head. One of the lads standing nearest to Robin was laughing, so Robin, thinking he was the culprit, just whacked him in the head and put him in a collar for two weeks. That's how short his fuse was.

Staying in a hotel during the week and travelling back to London at weekends, Friday would board the train to Cardiff, knock on locked toilet doors pretending to be the guard and, when the ticket was passed under the door, he would stroll off with it. Equally eventful was his début for Cardiff, a New Year's Day home game against Fulham. Fulham at the time boasted a star-studded team including George Best and Bobby Moore so the game drew Cardiff's biggest crowd of the season, most of whom had come to see George Best in action. However, the disappointment of Best's late withdrawal due to injury was soon forgotten when Friday got going.

South Wales Echo, 3 January 1977
Cardiff City 3 Fulham 0
. . . Robin Friday fired in two goals to help Cardiff City to a fine 3–0 win over Fulham at Ninian Park on Saturday. Afterwards he said: 'I'm going to like Cardiff and I'm looking forward to scoring a lot more goals . . .' His challenges for possession were at times over-robust and involved him in heated exchanges with John Lacey and Bobby Moore . . . Friday's first goal four minutes before the break stemmed from a great break by Evans . . . His second goal was a gem. . . From a neat Evans pass he wasted no time in angling a 15-yard ground shot off the outside of his right boot . . . Friday would have completed his hat-trick if he hadn't been pulled down by a rugby-style tackle . . .

MAURICE EVANS: My son Steven was a fanatical footballer and wanted desperately to be a professional. He wasn't quite good enough, though. He liked a good time, a little bit like Robin. I said to him, 'You'll never make a pro because you always want to do the things that pros shouldn't be doing – like staying out until four in the morning.' He said, 'What about Robin Friday?' I said, 'Robin will be finished very early.' He said, 'Rubbish, he's the best player that Reading has ever had.' So Robin got transferred to Cardiff and on New Year's Day my son said to me, 'You'll never guess who I saw last night dancing on the table in the Boar's Head?' I replied, 'Yeah, I can guess and there you are, he's just been transferred and look what he is doing.' Then, of course, what happened is that he goes out for Cardiff, scores two goals and turns Bobby Moore inside out that very morning. I thought, 'Christ – perhaps I am wrong.'

SHEILA FRIDAY: We went up on his début. It was snowing. We thought it would be called off.

ROD LEWINGTON: The Friday before his first match for Cardiff he was in the Boar's Head and at about nine o'clock the landlord, Dick Smith, said to him, 'Robin, why don't you make that your last one. Go home, get a good night's sleep and go down to your new club tomorrow.' Robin had been there since six in the afternoon. He said, 'Yeah, I think I will, Dick.' He drank his beer and said, 'Oh Dick, give us a dozen Colt 45s to take away.' You can be sure he drank them all that night and then went and scored two goals on his début.

PAUL WENT: He had a phenomenal début against Fulham – he gave everyone the runaround. He really did look a world-beater. I think he was keen to make an impression and it just showed what he was capable of when he set his mind to it. I don't think Bobby Moore knew what had hit him that day. Robin was turning him inside out, running him all over the park. I remember he squeezed Bobby's nuts – that was just Robin in a playful mood, there was no malice intended. I've actually seen him kiss a defender at a corner. Everyone would be lined up waiting for the ball to come in and Robin would turn round and kiss his marker on the cheek or on the lips or whatever, and it would completely throw the bloke. An elbow or a bit of shirt-tugging you can handle, but when a dirty great centre-forward with long hair turns round and kisses you, it can put you right off your game – and of course Robin knew that.

HARRY PARSONS, CLUB OFFICIAL: Bobby Moore was absolutely livid. He completely lost his rag and was chasing Robin all over the park after that. Bobby never usually lost his cool but I don't think he'd ever come up against anyone quite like Robin.

South Wales Echo, 3 January 1977
Robin Friday says: 'I did not find Fulham's defence any tougher than some of the sides I have played against for Reading. Standard-wise, there was not that much difference either, because Reading also play attractive football. But I was especially pleased to beat Fulham. After they had beaten Everton on their way to the FA Cup final, they were on the same train as the Reading team returning home. We were travelling second class while they were first class, and I was choked when the train steward opened the bar for Fulham after refusing our similar request. But on Saturday we were a class above Fulham.'

TONY FRIDAY: When he played that game he came back to me that night. I was playing for a team called Old Etonians and they had a clubhouse and he came straight back from Cardiff that night because he was still living in Acton. We were all well pleased because he got two on his début so he was full of himself that night.

CHARLIE HURLEY: I got a phone call from Jimmy Andrews on the Monday. 'Oh, Charlie,' he said, 'he was magnificent. He tore them inside out. He grabbed Bobby Moore by the balls and Moore was chasing him all over the place.' He went on and on and I let him ramble because I knew Robin inside out. Finally, I said, 'But, Jimmy, you've only had him for four days.' 'Ah,' he said, 'but he's a real gem.' I said, 'Give it a few months.'

ALF FRIDAY: We saw the Fulham game, we saw Carlisle, we saw Burnley. Robin didn't play that many games but I thought he played brilliant. He looked good in that class. They were in the Second Division and I remember this geezer saying to me, 'Robin's three moves ahead of them.'

South Wales Echo, 20 January 1977
Cardiff City 2 Stourbridge 0, Welsh Cup fourth round
. . . Robin Friday netted with a spectacular overhead kick but was rightly pulled up for offside . . . In his first Welsh Cup-tie Man of the Match Robin Friday set a fine example with his accurate use of the ball . . . He is the most powerful raider Cardiff have had . . . He's an aggressive striker with brilliant control and is sure to upset many Second Division defences.

PHIL DWYER: I used to give him a lift now and then. No one else would have him in their car but he was always fine with me. Similarly, I don't think anyone was too keen to have him as a room-mate. On away trips he was so bubbly and so full of life. We used to pick him up from the side of motorways and drop him off on motorways. We'd say to him, 'Do you want to be dropped off at a hotel or a service station?' and he'd just say, 'No, this will do me,' and he'd jump off at the side of the motorway. We never knew where he was heading. I don't think he ever did either. In all his time at Cardiff I never saw him drive a car or get into another vehicle apart from my car or the team bus.

ALF FRIDAY: Everything seemed to go wrong when he moved to
Bristol. We lost contact with him apart from going to the games.
We went to that last game – who was it against? They had to get
a draw.

SHEILA FRIDAY: Charlton?

ALF FRIDAY: No, Charlton is where he broke his cheekbone.
Peacock did it. Don't you remember? We were in the players' bar
and Tony Evans came up and told us Robin had had to go to the
hospital because of his cheekbone.

South Wales Echo, 24 January 1977
Cardiff City 1 Charlton 1
. . . Cardiff City manager Jimmy Andrews today demanded greater
protection for his striker Robin Friday who will be out of action with
a fractured cheekbone sustained in Saturday's match against
Charlton . . . 'Robin seems to be a marked man by opponents and
referees. He has been knocked from pillar to post and has taken so
much stick for us but he never complains about the rough treatment
and just gets on with it. But he keeps getting his name taken and
receives little protection from referees. The injury was caused by an
elbow smashed into Friday's face,' alleged Mr Andrews . . . 'Robin
reacted to a challenge and that's what has caused him to have his
name taken. He was in a daze and seeing stars, yet he played on in
great pain for 70 minutes. He was in considerable discomfort
yesterday.' . . . Andy Nelson, the Charlton manager, claimed, 'Friday
deliberately kicked Curtis. The referee booked Friday but if he had
seen the incident he should have sent him off. The referee was
intimidated by the Cardiff crowd.' Referee Shapter disclosed that he
did not book Friday for deliberately kicking an opponent but for
ungentlemanly conduct . . . No disciplinary action will be taken
against Friday for his late arrival to the match . . . He did not turn up

until 20 minutes before kick off . . . Robin was let down on a lift to Cardiff . . . He dashed to the railway station but missed the Cardiff train . . . Said Jimmy Andrews, 'His wife phoned to say what had happened and said Robin would get to Ninian Park in time for the kick-off. I kept him on the team-sheet which I had to hand to the referee 30 minutes before kick-off. A friend drove him to Cardiff and he is eager to move to South Wales and we are trying to fix him up with a flat as quickly as possible . . .'

LIZA FRIDAY: By the time we got to Bristol he was on the way down, really.

SYD SIMMONDS: I think he was interested in joining a better club but he knew that he would have to toe the line. Jimmy Andrews tried to calm him down, but obviously it never worked.

South Wales Echo, 11 February 1977
. . . Robin Friday, who was fined for his late arrival at Cardiff City's last home match, returns to the attack against Oldham Athletic tomorrow as City hope to check their slide towards the danger zone . . . Manager Jimmy Andrews fined Robin Friday for failing to arrive at the Charlton game until 20 minutes before kick-off . . . 'It was a bit unfortunate,' said Mr Andrews. After taking everything into consideration, he decided 'it should cost him a few bob' . . .

CHARLIE HURLEY: I'm not sure when it was but it couldn't have been more than a few months after he'd signed for Cardiff, and suddenly here's Robin in my office. 'Hello, boss,' he said – he still called me boss. I said 'Hello kid, you're not doing too bad up there are you, son?' 'Nah,' he said, 'I can't play for that little bastard. You're the only one I can play for. I've got to come back to you. You're the one who seems to be able to get me right. Can I come back to you?' I said, 'That's a nice compliment but we cannot pay thirty grand for you. You get a free transfer and I'll have you. But we can't pay the money.' He disappeared and I never saw him again.

South Wales Echo, 9 March 1977
Sheffield Utd 3 Cardiff City 0
. . . Just before half-time Friday ran off the field because of chest congestion . . . He returned briefly but withdrew himself within five minutes of the restart . . .

DR LESLIE HAMILTON, CARDIFF CITY CLUB DOCTOR: He seemed a very fit lad and there was no inkling of any medical problem with him at that particular time. I later learned that he was an asthmatic, he had an inhaler and would take puffs of it occasionally though it didn't seem to bother him that much. But he never mentioned the asthma when I examined him. No one at Reading did either.

South Wales Echo, 28 March 1977
Cardiff City 0 Plymouth Argyle 1
'Robin has fine skills and can be as unorthodox as Rodney Marsh but playing well is only part of the job for a forward. The most important part is scoring goals,' said Mr Andrews . . .

PAUL WENT: I had every respect for him as a player. He had unbelievable skills, absolutely phenomenal. His left foot was sublime. He could pull the ball down and crash it into the top corner of the net from 40 yards – I saw him do that in training many a time. He was also tremendous at shielding the ball. He'd put his head in where no one with any sanity would put their boot – he was the archetypal centre-forward. He was brilliant at running with the ball at people. He was a big guy but had so much skill he used to terrorise defences when he was going at them. If someone had got hold of him at 16 or 17 and taken him under their wing to try and curb that temper he would have been an England international without doubt. He could well have been one of the biggest talents this country has ever produced – a truly world-class star. Believe me, on his day there was no one better, he would just take your breath away. I'd have hated to have had to play against him on a regular basis. I had enough trouble coping with him on that one occasion.

South Wales Echo, 7 April 1977
Hereford Utd 2 Cardiff City 2
. . . Cardiff City striker Robin Friday faces a possible three-match suspension after being sent off during City's 2–2 draw with Hereford . . . Friday, whose playing career has been surrounded by controversy, got his marching orders in the 68th minute when he received his second caution of the match . . . City manager Jimmy Andrews said the club were considering fighting Friday's case . . . 'Hereford kicked the ball away when we were waiting to take a free-kick – a time-wasting tactic and an offence in itself. What incensed Robin was that the referee took no action. He told me that all he said to the referee was, "Get a hold of them, Ref." Doug Livermore the captain confirms that this is what he said.' Friday has now accumulated 28 penalty points this season, 14 since arriving at Cardiff in December . . .

South Wales Echo, 12 April 1977
Southampton 3 Cardiff City 2
. . . Cardiff City are now set to lose Man of the Match Robin Friday through suspension . . .

RITCHIE MORGAN: On the football pitch he was a complete one-off. I've never seen anything like the things he could do – he was fabulously gifted. He used to love taking the mickey out of the opposition. He'd nutmeg a defender and then laugh in his face. He'd pull his shorts down at them, show them his arse, give them two fingers – anything that would wind them up. Just his appearance would wind them up – the long scruffy hair, the shirt outside his shorts and that lazy walk he had. But all credit to him, he took a lot of stick. Defenders would kick him all over the park and he'd just laugh. Then he'd eventually whack them. We'd heard that at Reading once he'd got kicked throughout a game, eventually retaliated and got sent off. He was so annoyed at how he'd been treated that he went straight to the dressing-room and had a dump in the opposition's bath. A little welcoming present for when they came off the field.

South Wales Echo, 18 April 1977
Cardiff City 4 Luton 2
. . . Cardiff City striker Robin Friday, who is banned from Cardiff City's next two matches, gave a V sign to Luton goalkeeper Milija Aleksic after scoring the second of his two goals on Saturday . . . A minute earlier Friday had been lectured by the referee following a stormy incident with Aleksic . . . Intimidation seems to be a part of Friday's tactics for unsettling opponents but he denies that he deliberately courts trouble . . . 'I have a lot of skill and opponents don't like me taking the mickey out of them. They give me a lot of stick. Players go out of their way to kick me. You can only take so much when you're constantly kicked so I give it out as well. But I didn't go looking for aggro and I'm concerned with the bad reputation I've gained with referees. Some referees have got it in for me – before the match on Saturday the referee approached me and said, "I don't want any trouble today." I am not a villain but I do get involved because I am a winner. If you're not a winner it's not worth being in the game.'
   . . . Friday was forced to retire with a knee injury after 70 minutes which he claimed was caused by an Aleksic foul . . . 'The goalkeeper

came out with his foot up,' he alleged . . . Friday had been penalised for a high tackle on Aleksic in the 36th minute but when he held an outstretched hand in apology the goalkeeper reacted angrily . . . Seconds later Friday robbed a ponderous defender and gained ten yards to rifle a shot past Aleksic . . . After acknowledging the cheers of the crowd Friday turned towards the keeper and made the V sign . . . Asked about the gesture after the game, Friday said, 'I can't remember doing that.' Jimmy Andrews gave his reaction to the incident: 'I saw what happened and have had a word with him. I don't expect my players to behave like that on the pitch. It was completely unnecessary. After putting the ball in the back of the net no other gesture was needed towards the keeper. Part of the business of being a sportsman is self-discipline. If you can't keep control of yourself, you can't hope to control a ball. This type of conduct must be stopped.'

PAUL WENT: He was great in the dressing-room as well. His language didn't exactly come out of the Oxford Dictionary, but he loved a laugh and a joke. I remember many a time when we had an away match. We'd go away on the Friday night in our suits and ties and he'd turn up on the coach in a pair of jeans with the crotch missing, no pants, a scruffy T-shirt, winklepicker boots and a carrier-bag containing a bottle of Dry Martini. And that's a fact. I saw him turn up on match days like that. But nobody minded because of what he could do on the pitch. We all just accepted him like that. One of the directors was having a pop at Robin on the coach once and Robin threatened to crack him with the Martini bottle. There was no doubt he was going to let him have it, it took a few of us to calm him down – but that was Robin. He liked to get things sorted out there and then. God knows what would have happened if he'd have caught this director with the bottle, but he was deadly serious that he was going to do it. He was outrageous. I suppose the closest similarity would be someone like Frank Worthington. Frank was his own man like that. He had the long hair, would wear whatever he wanted, had a fantastic left foot and was a bit temperamental. But Robin was a terrific guy. Because underneath all this he had a heart of gold, and he was a genuinely lovely bloke who would do anything for you.

JIMMY ANDREWS: The young fans loved him. We had open days at the club and he was always the favourite. Kids love anyone who's out of order and a bit different. And of course he looked the part so to them it was a bit like meeting a TV star. He was great with them too, happy to sign autographs for as long as it took. He was also fiercely protective of the youngsters in the youth side. He didn't like anyone giving them a hard time and would always stick up for them.

PAUL WENT: He was so unpredictable. Some days we'd finish training and afterwards you'd go looking for him only to find him still out on the pitch with four or five of the 15-year-olds. He'd be knocking the ball about, shooting, chipping the keeper. I don't think he ever had any ambitions to play at a higher level, he just wanted to enjoy himself – it wouldn't have mattered to him whether he was playing at Arsenal, Man United, Reading or Cardiff, he was just content to play his football and give it his all. He was peculiar in the dressing-room. He could take a bollocking on the chin but his biggest hang-up seemed to be when the manager would have a go at younger players. He'd step in and fight their corner and would take any criticism of them almost as a personal affront.

JIMMY ANDREWS: I remember we were playing Carlisle in the last game of the season. We had to avoid defeat to avoid being relegated. We were hanging on for a draw when, in the last minute, our keeper was bundled over, the ball was played back across goal with the keeper desperately trying to recover his ground. There was a bit of a mêlée and all I can remember is seeing Friday charging back into our box, and believe me that's one place where you didn't want to see him at the best of times. And I just remember saying out loud, 'Oh Christ!' Because when you saw him in there you just knew that someone was going to go flying and you'd concede a penalty. He came steaming in just as the ball had been cleared off the line by our centre-half. The ball fell between one of their forwards and Friday took an absolutely massive swing at the ball but somehow managed to miss it and also managed to miss the forward. He swiped so hard at the ball he twirled round in mid-air about three times. It was cartoon stuff but, Jesus, if he'd connected with the player it was a definite penalty. Remember this is in the last minute of the last game of the season and we're hanging on to avoid relegation. Seeing him charge back there like a wild animal was one of the scariest moments of my life.

SHEILA FRIDAY: That night we was all drunk – oh, the drinks. One of the directors said, 'This is great.' Alf said, 'Yeah, it is, you're paying for it.' I'll tell you what I remember: when Cardiff played Chelsea and Robin had that Afghan coat on and they all came out in their blazers and he had that on. I thought, 'Oh my God.'

After having contributed to keeping Cardiff in the Second Division, scoring seven times in that season, Friday then went missing in the first of what would be many disappearances.

PAUL WENT: He was a ladies' man. It didn't matter what he was wearing, the women used to flock round him. He just had this aura about him. The rough-and-ready look went down a storm. But he wasn't really bothered about it. As far as women were concerned, his pulling technique seemed to consist of giving off an impression of mild disinterest which, of course, made them love him even more. He'd talk to everyone in the same manner. And that's why the supporters loved him – because he'd always give them the time of day and stop for a chat. He was just a very likeable rogue.

> *Having failed to turn up for pre-season training, Friday was reported to be in a London hospital suffering from a mystery virus. Worried by an illness that caused him to lose two stone in weight, Friday confessed, 'The doctors have told me I am suffering from dysentery but they are baffled as to why I am not making a full recovery. I am unable to eat and I feel terrible.' As suddenly as he had disappeared, Friday returned to Cardiff and reported for training. He now claimed that he'd been suffering from hepatitis, but medical tests proved negative. Manager Andrews told a local reporter, 'You're not going to believe this but somebody called Friday has just been in to see me looking like the fittest player in the world.' Friday reluctantly agreed to the manager's demands that he move from his Bristol home to live in Cardiff.*

JIMMY ANDREWS: I could never find him because he was supposed to be living in Bristol and I'd turn up and there would be about 25 milk bottles on the doorstep. Every weekend he'd disappear back to London, straight after the game.

South Wales Echo, 28 October 1977
. . . A 13-strong party left today for Brighton, including striker Robin Friday who has been out of the first-team scene since the beginning of the season suffering from a mystery virus . . .

PAUL WENT: Jimmy Andrews was a relatively quiet fella and

couldn't really control Robin so it was left to us out on the pitch to keep an eye on him. He really needed a strong disciplinarian to keep him in check, someone for him to look up to.

JIMMY ANDREWS: He'd often prowl about outside my office like a bear when he wanted something – usually a few bob to get him to London.

DR LESLIE HAMILTON, CARDIFF CLUB DOCTOR: He was such a like-able character, he almost hypnotised me. He was such a charismatic person that he could really fool you. He was the kind of person that you just had to like. You didn't want to say no to him. Having learned of his reputation at Reading, I said to Jimmy Andrews one day, 'Why on earth did you buy him?' He said, 'Well, I thought I could discipline him, get him into line.' Well, poor old Jimmy Andrews, he was a hell of a nice chap and we used to work well together, but he was never a disciplinarian and he completely failed with Robin Friday.

RITCHIE MORGAN: He always struck me as a quiet individual. He'd have a pint after the game and then he'd disappear. It was all part of his lifestyle – he'd just amble off and you wouldn't see him till the next Wednesday.

Friday's behaviour became increasingly bizarre. Staying in a hotel after an away defeat, Cardiff players were woken in the middle of the night by a terrible crashing noise. Venturing downstairs, they found Robin standing on the snooker table in just his underpants, hurling snooker balls around the room in true rock'n'roll fashion.

PHIL DWYER: I remember the snooker table incident. It was in a hotel the night we'd lost a Welsh Cup-tie. Robin went absolutely berserk, hurling balls around the room, breaking things. I think it was just his way of getting his frustration out. We just thought, 'Oh God, let's get him back to bed.' You didn't hang around when Robin was in that sort of mood.

PAUL WENT: I've known Robin to come off the pitch after a game and just get dressed and go home. He wouldn't even bother to have a shower. He'd just get dressed, take his carrier-bag with his dry Martini and he'd go – no explanation. He just did whatever he wanted to do. He loved his football, he knew he had ability but he just loved living life to the full. He lived for the day. He was never into talking about other players; he wasn't bothered about that or tactics.

PHIL DWYER: Watching him at close quarters, he was exceptional. If he got the ball and ran at you, you had no hope, he honestly could have taken on any defender in the world and turned him inside out. It was all a question of what sort of mood he was in and if he could be bothered. It was great to have someone like Robin in your team because you knew that when he was in the line-up you'd have a centre-forward *and* a centre-half: not only would he be up there running them ragged, but when it broke down he'd be the first person to start tackling back and try to win the ball back, which is unusual for someone of his skill level. So, as a centre-half, you'd get a bit of a breather before the ball was pumped back in. There was definitely a different feel to the team when Robin was in it.

CLIVE THOMAS, FIFA REFEREE: Robin was a hot-head all right. What you really needed to do was book him before the start of the game – then you'd both know where you stood.

South Wales Echo, 31 October 1977
Brighton 4 Cardiff City 0

... Inevitably the post-mortems of this match will be centred on the sending-off of Robin Friday whose long-awaited first appearance of the season was ended after 54 minutes by the referee ... City manager Jimmy Andrews launched into a blitzkrieg attack on referees in general and on Mr Robinson of Portsmouth in particular as he attempted to justify another violent flash of temper from the controversial striker ... Friday, fouled by Mark Lawrenson, retaliated with a kick which caught the defender in the face ... It was an ugly incident and whatever the pros and cons of what had gone on before, the referee cannot be faulted for sending him off ...

South Wales Echo, 31 October 1977

'Referees and opponents are waging an unfair war against Robin Friday,' said Jimmy Andrews. 'Friday will be fined for the offence but I do feel sympathy for him. It's a known thing that other teams go out to provoke him. They know what he's like so they just keep whacking him. He has a reputation and referees are looking for him before he starts. I told him before the game what would happen. I said, "They will kick you and hope that you retaliate," and that's how it turned out. On the first two occasions that the ball was played to him he was whacked from behind. Even when he was sent off, it was all started by a bad tackle from Lawrenson.' Alan Mullery, the Brighton manager, disagreed: 'The foul by Friday was one of the worst I have ever seen. He kicked my player in the face when he was on the ground! How can you defend that sort of behaviour?'

TONY FRIDAY: The last game he played was against Brighton and he got sent off. Mark Lawrenson was playing for Brighton then and Robin gave him a roasting. He kept doing him, but he did him once too often and the geezer did something so Robin turned round and whacked him. That was his last game for Cardiff.

> *By the time the final whistle had gone Friday had already left the ground and disappeared.*

South Wales Echo, 1 November 1977
'I am sick and tired of it,' said Jimmy Andrews. 'We waited a long time for the player to get back into action. To be sent off in his first game back is as much as a man can stand.'

TONY FRIDAY: He came back after that but then he went AWOL and he wasn't turning up for training.

South Wales Echo, 2 November 1977
City manager Jimmy Andrews has said Robin Friday will be dealt with for breach of contract as well as for being shown the red card. Friday had left Brighton's ground by the end of the match and City's firebrand striker also faces action from the Welsh FA for collecting 20 disciplinary points. After failing to report for training, Mr Andrews commented, 'He's in breach of contract and he will have to pay the price – and it will be a high price.'

> *In the space of a week, he'd been transfer-listed, fined £100 and suspended for three matches. Andrews stressed that 'he had been punished for an accumulation of disciplinary offences'. In his short explosive career at Cardiff, Friday had been booked 20 times – one in every eight appearances.*
>
> *On 20 December 1977, Robin Friday walked into Jimmy Andrews' office and announced that he was quitting the game for good. With Liza starting divorce proceedings against him, Friday again returned to London where he found work as an asphalter and decorator.*

JIMMY ANDREWS: He would often disappear for weeks at a time but he would always come back full of apologies, giving me that lovely big smile. And we always welcomed him back because we knew what he was capable of on the pitch – and the fans loved him.

RITCHIE MORGAN: His lifestyle was the only thing that stopped him from becoming one of the truly great players. I look back and I wonder how far he could have gone. You have to remember at this time he was really going off the rails. We were in the Second Division (as it was then), and not a particularly good side it has to be said, and yet he still turned in some terrific performances. You hear stories of wasted talent all the time but I never saw anyone with as much talent as Robin. If everything else in his life had been in the right place who knows what would have become of him.

DR LESLIE HAMILTON: When I saw Robin play, I used to ask myself, 'Here is a brilliant player' – because he was, there's no doubt of that, yet he'd played in Reading which is near a lot of the big London clubs, and I thought, 'Well, why haven't they snapped him up? It's not far to go for any London scouts. Why have Cardiff been able to get him?' And it was obviously because they were scared off by his reputation. It was such a terrible waste, really.

I can picture him now, out on the pitch, long hair flowing, cutting in from the wing, beating two or three players. I can remember him very vividly and I can't say that about too many players. He really was outstanding. His ball control was absolutely fabulous – I've never seen anything quite like it. It was such a shame because he had all the skills. There's no question he could have played for England if he'd sorted his head out. Robin was always very fit, which was surprising, really, considering his lifestyle. He never complained about injuries. The whole time he was at Cardiff, I can't ever remember having him on the table for any injury. I went back through my notes from the '70s and there's no record of him having any treatment. He used to throw himself around in matches and training and obviously picked up bumps and knocks, but he never complained about them. He was a real toughie. I know that he was very competitive in training and would treat it like a game. I never actually saw him in action on the training field but I saw the results of his efforts by the queue of players in my treatment-room afterwards.

JOHN CROOKS, CARDIFF CITY HISTORIAN: His disciplinary record was shocking. But he was one of those players whose career came and went in a blaze of glory – scoring twice on his début, then getting sent off and walking straight out of the ground and out of the club. I think a lot of people were naïve about the drug situation and just didn't realise what was going on. He was a phenomenal footballer, no doubt. And he looked the part as well. I watched him on several occasions and he'd do some things on the pitch that would absolutely take your breath away. And then he'd go and nut a defender.

The Flowers, the Footballs
and the Football Scarves

TONY FRIDAY: When I was playing for Old Etonians, Robin said he would come over and watch me – this is when he had finished at Cardiff and he had finished with Liza and he was living with my mum. We're playing, and all of a sudden, I see Robin walking over and he is well moxied. The keeper puts the ball down for a goal-kick and Robin runs on the pitch and kicks the ball. Now this club was a bit hoity-toity, it wasn't really our scene, it was just that one of our mates had got in there. They didn't like it but they knew we were good players so they couldn't say anything . . .

. . . The first team he went to play for after Cardiff was Hillingdon Borough. They were in the Southern League then and the manager wanted to get Robin playing because he knew he was different class. So he went through the motions of trying to get his registration but Cardiff wouldn't release it. They had paid that money and Robin had only played a certain amount of games. At the time, I was playing for this team in the Middlesex League, North Greenford. Robin knew them all and our manager, Chris Beck, said, 'Play up here and I'll try and get the registration sorted out.' So Robin comes up to watch a game and we won – it was a good game actually. Chris was saying, 'Get Robin to play and we're going to be the right business here.' So we're in the clubhouse at night having a few drinks and it's the same old story: Robin has gone and banged a geezer who is on the committee. Robin didn't know who the guy was. Anyway, all of a sudden, Brentford contacted him somehow and he went training with them. He was looking good, they got him fit – pre-season it was – and then all of a sudden he went on the missing list again. That was the last time he ever tried to play a good standard of football . . .

. . . I used to give him roofing work. We had some right laughs. You can imagine what it was like – me and him never stopped arguing. You'd take him to work and say, 'Do that Robin, will ya?' Of course all he's looking for is the easiest way to do the least possible work. We had a right laugh. There'd be me looking to nick all the lead and Robin trying to skip off. The guy who we used to work for, George, he couldn't believe Robin. Robin had him under his thumb. He was shit-scared of Robin. George was a tight arse: he'd knock people for their wages but he never knocked Robin. Robin went back to asphalting for a couple of years then and he was doing all right . . .

. . . He got married again. Mary. That was another time when I was inside. He'd been married three times and for two of them I was doing bird – so that was another wedding I missed, another wife I didn't know. He lived over in Fulham with her. It was about 1980 when they got married and he was only with her two or three years, top whack. I was living over at Fulham at the time, too. Then he ended up with another bird over there, Linda . . .

. . . He was in St Stephen's Hospital in Fulham Road and one day this nurse comes in and says she remembered his name. So the next day her mate comes up to see Robin and he was copping for her for a while. Then he ended up with that other girl, Linda. But at the time he was getting on the heavy stuff again. And this bird couldn't stand it so in the end I had him living with me and my girlfriend. Anyway, he was driving me and my bird apart. I said to him, 'You'll have to go to mum's or something cos this is no good.' Me and my girlfriend would be rucking [about Robin] and I would be saying, 'He's all right,' and then I'd turn around and Robin would have done something and I'd think, 'Oh no!' I mean he didn't even know what he was doing most of the time. He went back to live with my mum and he was working with me when I could give it to him. It was a waste of time having him because he would never do anything you told him to. He was looking to skive the whole day. He could graft but at the end of the day he was only getting X amount of pounds and people aren't gonna knock their bollocks off for peanuts. Towards the end my mum and dad got him a flat from a housing association back in Acton because basically he was getting on top of them. He was all right when he first moved in. He met another bird, Hazel. She lived with her sister and she used to stay with him at the weekends. He was in there six or seven months . . .

. . . We had a ruck over my mate Ricky from Reading. He was working with me and Ricky said something to Robin and he was in a right mood. So he hit Ricky with a lump of wood and broke his arm! I said to him, 'What the fuck are you doing? We're mates.' He said, 'Oh, fuck off, you two cunts,' and went home. I had to take my mate to hospital. I had the right hump about it. This was on the Friday morning. On Friday night, Robin calls and says, 'Where are my wages?' I didn't speak to him for about a week after that and I don't like that. So I phoned him on the Sunday and said, 'You all right? Come on. I'll pick you up and we'll go and have a light ale, me and you and your bird.' And I'm so glad I did that. Anyway, we had a right laugh about it. He said, 'How's Ricky?' and he was genuine about it. It tormented him that he done it. He used to torment himself. And that's what he was like. The next weekend he was down the club we used to go to, and there was a bit of a ruck, nothing serious, a bit of verbal, no fisticuffs. Hazel, his bird, ran out on the road and got hit by a car so he had to take her to hospital. I think that caused ructions between them . . .

. . . I was trying to contact Robin because I had a job to do and

I was gonna give him a day's work. I was gonna give him a couple of quid for Christmas. I thought he could help me with this job – it was only a couple of hours and I was gonna give him a oner [£100]. On the Friday before you break up for Christmas I would always go down to Acton and have a drink with my old mates. I went round this Friday to say, 'Come and help me with this job because it will give you a few quid for Christmas.' He wasn't doing a lot at the time. Hazel, his bird, was working and he would have been going up to my mum's for dinner. So on the Friday I'm knocking on his door, thinking, 'Where the fuck is he?' But with Robin he could be anywhere so I didn't think nothing of it. I went home and tried to phone him. I went out and went round again but couldn't get any answer. Now I'm starting to think. So on the Saturday, I phone my mum and said, 'Have you heard from Robin?' She said no. But sometimes she used to think that no news is good news. Then I assumed he might be up the hospital seeing his bird who was still in there. He was on the 'script' so I thought the one place he would have been was at the chemist to get his prescription. I phoned them and they said, 'No, he's not been in for a couple of days.' And that's when we knew something was wrong. I thought he might have been nicked or something and lying in a cell. My mum phoned Acton Old Bill and they went round to his house and that's when it broke . . .

SHEILA FRIDAY: The Sunday before he died he looked so well. Normally we would have our dinner and I would put Robin's and Hazel's in the oven because they liked to go for a drink. Then they'd eat when they got back. But that Sunday I had to work because of Christmas so I said to him, 'We'll all eat together.' Wasn't it funny that night? You said how well he looked that night as well, didn't you, Alf? And that was the last time I saw him. I spoke to him on the phone but I never saw him again.

Reading Evening Post, 31 December 1990

Former Reading football hero Robin Friday, who thrilled crowds with his wild-boy image, has died at the age of 38. The coroner has been informed about his death and an inquest is to be held. Friday's life was a tragic riches-to-rags story of a brilliant young star in the George Best mould who never reached his full potential. The cause of his death remains a mystery, but throughout his time at Reading he was well known for his heavy-drinking lifestyle. He was also thought to be asthmatic. He is thought to have collapsed at his home in Ealing. The funeral will take place at Ruislip crematorium on Friday. Former Reading coach Maurice Evans, now the general manager of Oxford United, said he would never forget Robin Friday. Mr Evans said, 'I mean it when I say Friday was the best player I've ever been involved with. He had an unbelievable talent, a tremendous player. He was difficult to handle because he did his own thing both on and off the field. The crowd loved him and so did I. I'll never forget him.'

Friday was signed by Reading after he played against them for a non-league heat in an FA Cup-tie. Mr Evans said Friday's career petered out soon after he joined Cardiff City in 1976. Stewart Henderson, a former team-mate, said, 'He had a great rapport with the crowd. He was a bit of an entertainer and a real fans' favourite. I had no contact with him at all after he left Reading.'

Friday scored 57 goals in his 135 games for Reading and was booked 20 times and sent off once between February 1974 and December 1976. He was voted Player of the Season by fans in 1974–75 . . .

Reading Evening Post, 2 January 1991

Reading football fans will never forget the day flamboyant Royals star Robin Friday celebrated a goal by kissing a policeman. That incident was just one of many antics which made Friday one of the most popular stars ever to play for Reading FC. His football skills were as legendary in local circles as was his taste for the good life, but his life was tragically cut short last week when his twin brother Tony found Robin dead at his West London flat. Paying tribute to Friday this week was ex-Reading manager Charlie Hurley, the man who signed Friday from non-league Hayes in 1974. Mr Hurley said, 'He was a character to say the very least and he was an exceptionally skilled player. I was fortunate to get him for Reading. The fans loved him not only because he was skilled but because he was very brave and very funny on and off the field.' Mr Hurley's most memorable moment was when Reading faced Rochdale in an end-of-season clash in 1975: 'Friday had just scored the winning goal with seconds to go in the match. He ran off the field and behind the goal and up to this policeman. He calmly removed the policeman's helmet and planted a kiss on his forehead. The crowd went hysterical. It's a moment I'll never forget,' he said. The following day the *Evening Post* ran a cartoon with a line of policemen waiting for their kiss from Friday. Mr Hurley added, 'He had a tough old life and he always said that playing for Reading was one of the happiest times of his life. He always gave 100 per cent and he will be sadly missed by anyone who ever saw him play.'

Former *Post* sports editor Dave Dibben remembers the wild but gentle side of Friday. Mr Dibben explained how Friday experienced a turbulent youth and was always in trouble with the law and he recalled many anecdotes of Friday's behaviour whilst playing for the Royals including tales of all-night drinking sessions and spending nights in police cells for riotous post-match antics. 'But beneath it all he really was a decent guy,' Mr Dibben said. 'Friday was one of the most skilled footballers to play for Reading since the Second World War. He certainly would have been an international if he had continued his career. It got to a point where people didn't come to see Reading, they came to see Robin Friday. He was like a one-man team.' Mr Dibben also recalls an amusing anecdote during a game against Rotherham at Elm Park. Barry Wagstaff is a player who left Reading for Rotherham and he was in the side that faced Reading that day. Friday and Wagstaff were friends and the two of them were waiting in the penalty area for a corner when Friday pulled Wagstaff's shorts down. That's what he was like.

Robin Friday was a regular feature in the Boar's Head pub in the town centre. Legend has it he could be seen quaffing ale just hours before big matches. Sports writers described him as a genius and a diamond and a one-in-a-million talent. He was completely unpredictable both on and off the field. A local official recalls the time Friday turned up late for a match at Hayes and the side started without him: 'I was linesman for the match. I remember Hayes started without him and played for the first ten minutes with ten men. That was the kind of respect they had for Friday. He had obviously been in the pub before the match and was staggering about the field. The opposition paid little attention to him until he blasted in the only goal of the match and did little else throughout the game.'

TONY FRIDAY: The funeral was marvellous. Starting with kids from our school, all the teams we had played for, plus Stan Bowles, Charlie Hurley, Steve Hetzke, Tommy Youlden – Robin used to drive him mad – and a lot of players from Hayes. It was a brilliant turn-out, it really was. There were people I hadn't seen for ages and ages – how they found out about it I just don't know.

CHARLIE HURLEY: The crematorium was packed. it was chock-a-block with the London lads, the nous boys, the ones who know what it's all about. Real characters.

LIZA FRIDAY: At the funeral I have never seen so many people. You couldn't see the grass. There were flowers and footballs and football scarves, but it was the amount of people that I couldn't believe. *Hundreds* of people. When we got to the flat, the stairs and the corridors leading to his mum's front door were packed with people. You couldn't get past anyone. It was a real tribute.

But I have to say they were all there with their crombies and their collars turned up – see them down a dark alley and you would really be sorry.

ARABELLA FRIDAY, ROBIN'S DAUGHTER: They were saying to us, if you ever need anything, this is my number. Don't hesitate to call.

LIZA FRIDAY: We should have taken a few of those numbers.

TONY FRIDAY: They recorded the day of death as 22 December but they couldn't be sure. The last time anyone had any contact with him was the Wednesday so he could have been dead from then. Hazel's sister was the last person to speak to him. Robin phoned Hazel's house (she lived with her sister) and she always said that he sounded funny. Basically that's how it all ended, which was completely tragic. It was devastating for the family. There's never a good time to lose someone, but two days before Christmas . . . I just couldn't believe it.

Reading Evening Post, 4 January 1991
The family of former Reading football hero Robin Friday could face an agonising month's wait before they learn of his cause of death. A spokesman for the west London's coroner's offices admitted that it could be as long as February before the cause of death is known. The body of the former soccer genius who fired the crowds with his wild-boy image was found in his flat in west London a few days before New Year. Family, friends and former colleagues of the 38-year-old are still in shock over his sudden death. Despite the delay in the cause-of-death enquiry, the funeral is expected to go ahead at Breakers Crematorium, Ruislip, at noon today. Cardiff City and Reading FC have sent flowers and condolences to the family. Tony Friday, who found the body said, 'My parents are still very, very upset. They are devastated. We don't know how he died, we are

waiting for the coroner's report.' He added, 'We last saw him a couple of Saturdays ago. I tried to contact him but he wasn't in. I thought he had taken himself off somewhere like he sometimes did. Then we got worried and went around to his flat in Ealing where we found him dead. We were terribly shocked.'

CHARLIE HURLEY: I'm glad that he touched my life. I was very sad when his brother phoned me up and told me. Very sad. Actually, I never knew he had a twin brother. I met him at the funeral. I said to him, 'Don't tell me there's another Robin Friday. Two of them! How did your mother and father survive the two of you? Are you as bad as Robin?' 'No, no,' he said, 'I'm worse.'

The Greatest Footballer
You Never Saw

Reading Evening News post-bag:
Why did they sell Friday? I had to write this letter because I am so angry about what I've just read in the *Evening Post*. Reading have sold our only footballer, Robin Friday, for a poor £30,000. Don't the so-called directors and Charlie Hurley know that he was the best player Reading have had for the last 20 years? I had been a fan all that time. They will lose 30,000 on the gates in a few games before they go down.

    Yours disgusted and no longer a supporter.

      D.J. Hatton

MAURICE EVANS: When I took over as Reading manager, the very first board meeting I went to, the chairman said to me, 'Maurice, I've got a petition here, got up by a police inspector with three thousand names on it, to bring Robin Friday back to Reading.' That was in 1978, my first board meeting.

Reading Evening Post, 3 January 1980
Maurice Evans, the Reading coach, picked a team of the '70s . . . Death, Hetzke, White, Bowman, Hicks, Wagstaff, Bewles, Kerning, Friday, Sanchez, Dunphy and sub Chapell.

MAURICE EVANS: Robin Friday was an unbelievable character, the most unbelievable character I've ever worked with. He would not take anything seriously and that was his biggest problem. In my opinion Robin could have played for England. If he had really set his mind to it and said, 'This is what I want,' he could have done it. But he loved the good times all the time and you can't do that when you are playing football. I remember pulling him aside one day and saying, 'Robin, if you would just settle down for three or four years you could play for England.' He said, 'Yeah, but I've had a far better time than you've ever had in your life.' I looked at him and replied, 'That may well be right.'

DAVID DOWNS, READING FC HISTORIAN: I did an article for the *Reading Evening Post* at the end of the '70s. It was an analysis of the club's decade and I had to select a player of the decade and obviously it was Robin Friday. If you asked anybody who had watched Reading since the war who was the one player they would remember more than any other, I think 99 out of 100 would answer Robin Friday.

JOHN MURRAY, READING PLAYER: Ability-wise, he could have played for England, no doubt about it.

Reading Evening Post, 5 January 1980
The '70s was probably the most turbulent decade in Reading's history and certainly one of the most interesting . . . It was a decade that opened full of hope as Jackie Mansell's free-scoring side threatened to take the Third Division by storm . . . and one that saw despair and disappointment before Maurice Evans's record-breaking triumph at the end of 1979 . . . In 1971 all hopes were dashed when the club were relegated to the Fourth Division . . . It took Reading five years to climb out . . . The decade saw many Reading players appear in the colours . . . But without doubt the character of the decade has to be Robin Friday, that flamboyant colourful character who graced the Elm Park stage for a regrettably short time . . . He

knocked in 53 goals for the club, but more than that he delighted the fans with his skills and cheek . . . He scored what to me was the most memorable goal of the decade . . . It came in a tension-packed 5–0 win against Tranmere Rovers on 31 March 1976 as both sides raced for promotion . . . Reading led by two goals at half-time before Robin struck . . . He received the ball with his back to goal on the edge of the area, hoisted it over his head with his foot, spun round and slammed it in the back of the net in one graceful movement . . . Even the referee, Clive Thomas, seemed moved by this moment of sheer skill that contributed to a magnificent win and helped Reading back into the Third Division . . .

CHARLIE HURLEY: Robin on the pitch was near enough the same as Robin off it. He was wild, he was carefree, a real free spirit as a player.

ROD LEWINGTON: Gary Peters, who played with Robin, always said that it was the accident that made Robin the way he was. He thought that Robin had come so close to death that he just wanted to live each day as it came and forget about tomorrow.

EAMON DUNPHY: I think that's right. I think that had a very profound effect on him. I think it was only his extraordinary strength that kept him alive after that.

MAURICE EVANS: I've played and worked with all sorts of players – great players like John Aldridge and Dean Saunders, inter-national goalscorers, top-quality players – and Robin, in many ways, had more than they did.

DAVID DOWNS: If he was playing nowadays when the refs are so much stricter he wouldn't have lasted half the game. He got booked a lot but in those days if you got booked you didn't get sent off. Nowadays you get booked and the slightest thing you do after that means you're off.

CHARLIE HURLEY: Robin would have loved to have played against Vinny Jones. You know what? Vinny Jones would have ended up with his legs tied together.

ROD LEWINGTON: Blair? Major? Ashdown? The only party Robin would have voted for was the Monster Raving Loony Party.

EAMON DUNPHY: I think he could have played for England if he'd had pace. He certainly could have been a Premiership player if he had been spotted earlier. Teddy Sheringham springs to mind when he played for Millwall a lot further forward than he does for Spurs. Robin looked like Mario Kempes although he didn't have the pace that the Argentinian had. Robin was one of those wonderful footballing forwards with great strength and a great eye for goal. The important thing for a player like that is to be able to turn, keep possession of the ball and beat people, and Robin could do all that.

CHARLIE HURLEY: I'd have loved to have played alongside him. Actually, maybe it would've been better if I'd played against him.

JOHN CROOKS, CARDIFF CITY HISTORIAN: When people down here heard about his death there was a lot of real sadness, despite all the problems he caused. I suppose it's because he was one of those characters who come along once in a lifetime.

CHARLIE HURLEY: All players are different. There are players who would turn it on for you at home and never do it away. There are other players, though, that would die for you no matter where you were. Robin was like that.

JOHN MURRAY: He was a great lad, but he was totally mad.

ROD LEWINGTON: If the guy was keen, had trained properly, conducted himself properly – say, if he had the mentality of a David Platt – he would have been a world-beater. People talk about Shearer today but Robin was twice as good. No one could touch his ball control, he had strength on the ball and he was unique. I've never seen a player like it before or since and I think anyone who regularly saw him play will tell you the same.

JOHN MURRAY: Maybe Robin wouldn't be a footballer with today's rules and regulations. He would probably have been a pop star.

CHARLIE HURLEY: I loved him. You must understand that wherever he went he would have touched someone's place, or club or house or whatever. He didn't just sit there. He was full of life and he always loved a laugh – very crude humour. The lads who weren't crude didn't like it, but you can't have it all. I'd tell everyone that: in life you can't have it all.

EAMON DUNPHY: He was a very lonely guy at the heart of it all. He was a lonely guy and he used to get very sad and sorry for himself. He wasn't a thug, he wasn't a lout. Robin was a very gentle, intelligent nice man. I think it got to him that people didn't think of him that way.

ALF FRIDAY: He was nice to his kids, really nice. He left them but he was still nice. It was just one of those things.

CHARLIE HURLEY: I would have thought that he crammed more into his 38 years than I have in my 60. He had a very full life, a very exciting life. But you have to remember that there is excitement you like and there is excitement that can frighten you to death.

JIMMY ANDREWS: He had incredible vision. And once he'd got the ball it was almost impossible to get it off him. He was a phenomenal goalscorer as well, so he really had everything – the complete centre-forward. If Alan Shearer is worth £15 million, I'd put Robin Friday, minus his temperament, right up there alongside him.

CHARLIE HURLEY: You've done me proud. The Reading fans have loved you and you have made your mark. Today when people talk to me about Reading they always, always mention Robin Friday. You know what, he'll be up there in heaven right now, looking down on me and saying, 'He's still a pain in the arse.' He's still telling the truth about me.

ROBIN FRIDAY (as quoted in the *South Wales Echo*): 'As a striker I take a lot of stick, so I give it out as well. On the pitch I hate all opponents. I don't give a damn about anyone. People think I'm mad, a lunatic. I am a winner.'